AFTER THE HANGOVER

THE CONSERVATIVES' ROAD TO RECOVERY

R. EMMETT TYRRELL JR.

THOMAS NELSON
Since 1798

NASHVILLE   DALLAS   MEXICO CITY   RIO DE JANEIRO

Published in Nashville, Tennessee, by Thomas Nelson. Thomas Nelson is a registered trademark of Thomas Nelson, Inc.

Thomas Nelson, Inc., titles may be purchased in bulk for educational, business, fund-raising, or sales promotional use. For information, please e-mail SpecialMarkets@ThomasNelson.com.

Library of Congress Control Number: 2010921729
ISBN 13: 9781595552723

Printed in the United States of America
10 11 12 13 14 WCF 9 8 7 6 5 4 3 2 1

For Jeanne
with Love and Gratitude

ALSO BY R. EMMETT TYRRELL JR.

Public Nuisances

The Future that Doesn't Work:
Social Democracy's Failures in Britain

Report on Network News' Treatment of the
1972 Democratic Presidential Candidates, ed.

The Liberal Crack-Up

Orthodoxy: The American Spectator's 20th
Anniversary Anthology, ed.

The Conservative Crack-Up

Boy Clinton

The Impeachment of William Jefferson Clinton
(with Anonymous)

Madame Hillary
(with Mark W. Davis)

The Clinton Crack-Up

The Best of The American Spectator's
Continuing Crisis

CONTENTS

CONTENTS

INTRODUCTION

Point of Clarification

In the book that you are about to read—with pleasure I hope and illumination—you will at some point become aware that I capitalize the words Liberal and Liberalism even as I invariably capitalize the word God. Please do not let this confuse you. It is not in deference to the Liberals' frequent assertions of their divine attributes that I make this typographical adjustment. Rather it is out of my recognition that today's Liberal is not a liberal. Consequently, I want to distinguish contemporary American Liberals from earlier liberals, who are known to history as classical liberals or nineteenth-century liberals.

Contemporary Liberals are so distinct from earlier liberals that I am not even certain there is an ancestral link. DNA samples are not readily available, but if they were I believe that, say, the late Senator Edward Kennedy's claim to an ancestral relationship with, say, James Madison or Thomas Jefferson, would be dismissed as illegitimate. Rather, it is we conservatives who can rightly claim ancestry reaching back to the Founding Fathers and beyond to Locke. Moreover, we need not go through the invasive process of procuring DNA samples. We can make our genealogical claim on the basis of shared principles, particularly our shared scruples about big government's threats to individual liberty and our shared enthusiasm for constitutionally limited government, the rule of law, and free markets that spread prosperity and preserve freedom. Also like the Founding Fathers we believe America is a blessed and exceptional nation.

Today's American Liberals are collectivists. Their equivalents found elsewhere in the world are socialists, though very few are sufficiently oblivious of the dreary socialist reality to admit to the designation. Even in times of economic uncertainty socialism remains very much out of fashion. Doubtless you have noticed the contemporary Liberals' indignant howls when they are accused of socialism for nationalizing large portions of the private sector or for imposing a nanny state on private citizens. They shun the term. Yet, today they are championing unprecedented peacetime government controls. If the Obama administration proposes high-minded regulations for the bristles in your toothbrush do not be surprised. Properly understood, that is not very liberal. Consequently, to avoid confusion between today's Liberals and true liberals I employ a capital *L*. Call it the scarlet letter.

A true liberal of the nineteenth-century variety, Sir William Harcourt made my point with elegance back in 1873 when he told a gathering at Oxford that "liberty does not consist in making others do what you think is right. The difference between a free Government and a Government which is not free is principally this—that a Government which is not free interferes with everything it can, and a free Government interferes with nothing except what it must. A despotic government tries to make everybody do what it wishes, a Liberal Government tries, so far as the safety of society will permit, to allow everybody to do what he wishes." [1]

Let me hasten to add that my deployment of the capital *L* is not original. William F. Buckley Jr. and his editors at the *National Review* devised this expediency at the dawn of the modern conservative movement in the 1950s. As Buckley explained in the Introduction to his 1959 book, *Up from Liberalism*, "I capitalize the words 'Liberal' and 'Liberalism,' by which I intend a pious gesture of historical deference to words (liberal, liberalism) that once meant something very different from what they have come to mean in contemporary American politics." [2] Yes, he joked, "pious gesture." From his earliest days in journalism, Bill employed humor and wit in his political commentary and polemics. The practice has continued among prominent conservative writers to this very day, thus giving humor and wit a bad odor with Liberals, and I believe explaining why their own commentary is usually devoid of these agreeable qualities. Surely at some level they must know that at least *some* political activity is a hoot. Well, perhaps not; Liberal politics seem often to be motivated by what members of the American Psychiatric

Association diagnose as free-floating anxiety or General Anxiety Disorder (GAD).

This explains the Liberals' creation of another phenomenon that you will encounter in this book, which I designated some years ago as *Kultursmog*. The term has gained acceptance among objective observers such as Tom Wolfe, except that he calls it "the social manipulation of 'the Good,' a subset of the sociology of concept construction," and dates it back to the Phoenicians in the fifth century B.C. Viewed from a more recent perspective, *Kultursmog* is the pollution of our culture by politics, almost exclusively Liberal politics. The Liberals' insistence on arrogating the word liberal despite their being the opposite of liberal is by now a commonplace example of *Kultursmog*. Later in this book I shall elaborate on the nature and noxious particulates of *Kultursmog*. For now, however, let me say that it is the only environmental hazard that remains untreated by government and unremarked by environmentalists—who themselves are leading contributors to the *smog*.

A historic revelation as to how the *Kultursmog* is made occurred late in 2009 when hackers broke into the electronic files of one of the world's leading Global Warmist research centers, the Climatic Research Unit (CRU) of the University of East Anglia in the United Kingdom, and posted some three thousand of the Warmists' conspiratorial e-mails and files for all the world to read. To my ineffable gratification, the e-mails displayed the Global Warmists sedulously engaging in just what you would expect in the

Kultursmog: deceits, distortions, and the suppression of dissenting points of view.

Now exposed on the Internet, adherents to the *Kultursmog*'s credo on Global Warming could be seen surreptitiously blacklisting and suppressing scientists who disagreed with them, the so-called "Global Warming skeptics." In one instance Michael Mann, director of the Earth System Science Center at Pennsylvania State University, e-mailed like-minded Global Warmists, advising them to isolate and ignore scientists and scientific journals that publish the views of the "skeptics." "I think we have to stop considering *Climate Research* as a legitimate peer-reviewed journal," he wrote, going on to urge the encouragement of "our colleagues in the climate research community to no longer submit to, or cite papers in, this journal." Now that is precisely how *Kultursmog* taints the debate.

Then there was Phil Jones, director of the University of East Anglia project. He e-mailed Mr. Mann and others to "delete any e-mails you may have had with Keith" regarding indelicate references to the UN's Intergovernmental Panel on Climate Change's Fourth Assessment Report. Another e-mail from Jones to a co-conspirator asked that he "change the Received date! Don't give those skeptics something to amuse themselves with." Also among the hacked e-mails was one from an unnamed scientist, urging his readers to "hide the decline" of temperatures in data that might indicate global cooling rather than Global Warming. His concern is understandable. At the time there had been no Global Warming for almost a decade, contrary to the

Global Warmists' computer predictions. In fact, from 2005 until the Global Warmists' e-mail conspiracy was exposed there had been global cooling!

Thanks to the work of these public-spirited hackers the world has been given abundant evidence that the Global Warmists are dishonest bullies. As for me, I have been given a perfect educational model to demonstrate how my discovery, *Kultursmog*, works. But this exposé is not without its melancholy aspects too. There once was a day when scientists were empiricists, believing in reason and fair play. Empiricism, reason, and fair play, of course, are some of the values observed by the original liberals and ignored by the Liberals of today.

RET
January 8, 2010
Old Town
Alexandria, Virginia

PRONOUNCED DEAD

The Premature Obituary of America's Longest Dying Political Movement

The 2008 presidential election has now been interred in history's cemetery for over a year. The little candles that once flickered around its gravesite burned down months ago. The election ended in a Democratic victory, not a landslide but close enough for the political pundits in their slovenliness to call it one and return to composing what through the decades has been a staple of mainstream journalism, the conservative movement's obituary.

The journalists' deathwatch began two years earlier with the Democrats' takeover of the 110th Congress, a takeover hastened by the Republicans' abandonment of fiscal restraint and by the scandals perpetrated by various minor Republican Congressional members and their political operatives. For the next two years, the political community produced murmurings of the conservative movement's "decline," its "fragmentation," its "exhaustion," and—without attribution—"the conservative crack-up." I say this without attribution because I coined the term in an

American Spectator symposium devoted to the troubled condition of conservatism during President Ronald Reagan's second term. Supposedly, conservatism has been cracking up for decades, and always conservatism's obituarists have been there in the parking lot, waiting for the hearse to pull up.

In 1992, I published a book titled *The Conservative Crack-Up* in which I pondered the conservative movement's troubles during the Reagan administration's last years. I also laid down a thesis about conservatives that was as true then as it is today: the conservative political animal is so fundamentally different from the liberal political animal that the two might be drawn from different species. Politically speaking, the conservative is more domesticated, less feral.

Liberals seemed to like the idea. In the *New York Times Book Review*, the book received a page-2 review, the *Review*'s silver medal for the week's literary competition. To review the book, the *Times*'s editor chose a former Reagan speechwriter, the conservative personality Peggy Noonan, whose review was more a psychoanalysis of me than a review of my book. She was almost Freudian in her analysis of my vocabulary, language admittedly more complicated than a speechwriter's, but then consider my clientele! Peggy's sly disparagement validated another of my propositions about conservatives, namely: conservatives, particularly conservative writers, have remained marginalized by the political culture and left with only one expedient to stardom, which is to snipe at fellow conservatives.

Sometimes it has worked, as in the spectacular rise of the early George Will. Sometimes it has proved futile, as in the ongoing, muddled career of Tucker Carlson. As we shall see in the pages ahead, for three decades the rat race has continued.

In my 1992 book, I dated the crack-up of the late Reagan years from July 1, 1987, when President Ronald Reagan stepped to the microphones and with ill-considered joviality nominated Judge Robert Bork to the Supreme Court. Throughout the subsequent confirmation hearings, the conservatives were utterly feckless in protecting Bork, despite the presence of a card-carrying member of the conservative movement in the Oval Office.

What ensued was a perfect example of the Liberal-conservative species variation. The Liberals snarled and clawed. The conservatives looked bemused. Bork's antagonists transmogrified him from the sensible, thoughtful federal Court of Appeals judge that he was, into a creep. Senator Edward Kennedy declared that "Robert Bork's America is a land in which women would be forced into back-alley abortions, blacks would sit at segregated lunch counters, rogue police could break down citizens' doors in midnight raids, school children could not be taught about evolution, writers and artists could be censored at the whim of government, and the doors of the federal courts would be shut on the fingers of millions of citizens."[1] Senator Howell Heflin was less verbose. He simply called Judge Bork "some kind of right-wing freak,"[2] who led "a strange lifestyle."[3] Ironically, Senator Heflin was a conservative Democrat from Alabama, who, when "down home," defended the right to bear arms and opposed both gay rights and abortion—that last issue being the chief stimulant that agitated Liberal neurosis over Bork.

Besides being a well-known judge, Bork had been a distinguished scholar at the Yale Law School. The conservatives' inertness in defending him exemplifies another of my propositions regarding conservatives: they do not do politics as well as Liberals. They can be energetic, resolute, unprincipled, and ad hominem, but rarely as energetic, resolute, unprincipled, and ad hominem as their Liberal opponents. Illustrative of the Liberals' political artistry is that they have convinced large numbers of ordinary Americans that the conservatives—not the Liberals— maintain a brutal "attack machine," and are adepts of "politics of personal destruction." Looking back at the Liberals' grotesque demonization of Bork, one has to be impressed by their powers of misrepresentation. No conservative with any claim to the respectability of a Kennedy or a Heflin has ever in modern times uttered slanders of such virulence. Any who attempted to would not survive in public life.

Historians may dispute me and date the conservatives' late-1980s adversity from the Iran-Contra unpleasantness, which made headlines on November 12, 1986, or from the 1986 midterm elections, when President Reagan's Republicans lost the Senate. Still, whatever history's judgment might be, from the late 1980s into the early 1990s the conservative condition remained parlous. Moreover, out on the hustings another Liberal miracle worker was making his way to the White House, cast in the heroic role originated by Franklin D. Roosevelt and updated by John F. Kennedy in 1960. This miracle worker, Governor Bill Clinton, was to vanquish President George H. W. Bush by using the same script developed by Roosevelt and edited by Kennedy. Both were models for what has become the prototypical Liberal president: always youthful, charismatic, bold, intellectual, all in all fundamentally irresistible. It is a model that has rather amazingly endured for eight decades.

After the Democratic victory of 2008, critics of the conservative movement warned that the Reagan model so often invoked by Republicans was now a thing of the past. Yet Liberals have been relying on the prototypical Liberal presidency for more than two generations. From time to time in this book, I shall propound the theory that Liberals remain petrified in a mythic past while conservatives have been intellectually dynamic, discarding ideas and prejudices held by earlier conservatives—say, President Herbert Hoover or Senator Robert A. Taft—and adopting alternatives, some once championed by the likes of Franklin Roosevelt and John F. Kennedy.

For instance, conservatives have moved from the isolationism of their political ancestors to what historians at the middle of the twentieth century called *internationalism*. Some conservatives have actually become evangelists of democracy, following the path of Kennedy and Roosevelt. Others remain more restrained in their foreign policy goals, standing only for the defense of American national interests. The split became apparent as the war in Iraq continued. At any rate, there are few isolationists numbered among American conservatives today. Nor are there many who remain in Senator Taft's tradition of strict budget balancers either. Most contemporary conservatives stand for growth. Taft's followers have been replaced by supply-siders. Yet the charge leveled against conservatives by Liberals is that they are slaves to orthodoxy, to an unchanging fundamentalism.

Over the years a few winsome attributes have been added to the model of the prototypical Liberal presidency. Amusingly, these additions require exertions from their presidential candidates that are often injurious to themselves and occasionally life threatening. By the 1970s the prototypical Liberal presidential candidate had to be physically fit and given to exercising in public, a requirement that almost killed Jimmy Carter during his only known 10K race. A decade later, the candidate also had to display military prowess, which explains why the diminutive governor Michael Dukakis allowed himself to be photographed popping out of the portal of an M1 Abrams tank, looking like a large toadstool, his tiny head topped by a huge helmet. The stunt ended his candidacy in an ambush of laughter.

Then in the early 1990s, Governor Clinton had to embrace all of the above, along with an implausible enthusiasm for rock music and for the more vulgar aspects of adolescent culture. He played a musical instrument onstage, and to an MTV audience of pimply-faced teenagers, confided his preference in underpants. Impelled by yet another requirement of the prototypical Liberal president, ethical purity, Clinton went over the top, promising "the most ethical administration in history." Almost immediately the skeletons began clattering in his closet, inspiring investigative reporters to pursue his history of dodgy land deals, recklessly financed gubernatorial campaigns, and, of course, his famed scortatory projects.

Clinton's arrival in the White House occasioned yet more prophecies of the conservative movement's demise. This would be the third round of obituaries for conservatism since the modern conservative movement's birth in the early 1950s. The first round came in 1964 (Goldwater). Then came the obituaries of 1974 (Nixon). Now we have blubbered through the Republican defeat of 2008 and the fourth round of obituaries for conservatism, which make it the longest dying political movement in American history. Yet the movement is still around, and oddly enough, the political center toward which Liberal political candidates claim they are running is more clearly shaped by modern American conservatism than by Liberalism.

When Ronald Reagan and George W. Bush each ran for the presidency, they forthrightly claimed they were for conservative policies, for instance, lower taxes and limited government. They publicly opposed abortion and promised to defend social issues and a strong foreign policy. When Bill Clinton and, later, Barack Obama ran for president, both were vague on these matters. They intoned the Liberal pieties—"Hope" and "Change"—but they certainly did not say they favored higher taxes and usually danced around the question of extending government's growth.

In other words, whereas Reagan and Bush spoke forthrightly, Clinton and Obama practiced deception. For their forthrightness, the conservative candidates were accused of ideological extremism. The Liberals' deference to the conservatively influenced center continued for President Obama even after his victory. As he presided over the largest peacetime expansion of government since the New Deal, he actually declared in his February 24, 2009, address to a Joint Session of Congress that he had done so "not because I believe in bigger government—I don't."[4]

The obituaries for conservatism that followed Clinton's election brought the term *conservative crack-up* back to life. Happy Liberals used it freely. Google the term and you will find that in the aftermath of the 1992 election, the term took on new life, usually employed by gloating Liberals but occasionally by conservatives. Even that famously sensible conservative, Charles Krauthammer wrote, "The conservative crackup is near."[5]

Actually, the long-standing pessimism accorded conservatism's prospects has always been unjustified and was for a certitude unjustified in 2008. As I just pointed out, conservatism has been a powerful force over the last few decades in shaping the *middle* of American politics. Moreover, from the last quarter of the twentieth century on, the Liberals have had more reason to feel endangered than conservatives.

From its overwhelming preponderancy at the end of the New Deal, Liberalism has had to witness a growing conservative movement that has at times routed Liberals. Even in 2008 the strength of conservatism forced the Democrats to draft moderate-to-conservative candidates to campaign in the South, the Heartland, and the West. The ascendancy that Liberals achieved with Clinton's election lasted only two years before the Democrats suffered a loss of historic proportions. Republicans captured both houses of Congress for the first time in four decades. Talk of conservative demise or crack-up subsided, not to be heard again for a dozen years. A dazed President Clinton was forced to declare, "The era of big government is over,"[6] a declaration as famous as his line "I did not have sexual relations with that woman, Miss Lewinsky" though less precise.[7]

The conservative movement's revival in 1994 was for a decade seen as irreversible—an indelicate little matter utterly forgotten after the Democrats' 2008 victory. It began with incoming Speaker of the House Newt Gingrich's seductive Contract with America. Though the Contract was only partially implemented, conservatism was strong enough to vanquish Clinton's vice president, Al Gore. Running on his boss's record of peace and prosperity, Gore should have won, but he was beaten by a relatively unknown governor, probably because Gore broke with his boss's centrism and veered too far left in the 2000 race. His opponent, governor George W. Bush, campaigned as a full-blown conservative, though in a gesture that demonstrated conservatism's lingering controversiality (at least, in the media), Bush confected the dubious label "compassionate conservative." The term was an early presentiment of Bush's political tin ear that would become evident as the Iraq War dragged on and his popularity declined. Nonetheless, the conservative tide remained on the rise in his first two years of office. In 2002 Bush became the first president since FDR to gain congressional seats in his first midterm election.[8]

By Bush's 2004 reelection, conservatism was so strong that the term *conservative crack-up* was now flung back at Liberals as a taunt. In 2005, Jonah Goldberg, the cheeky *National Review* writer, chided those few Liberal dreamers who might still be pondering "whether a 'conservative crack-up' is nigh."[9] Goldberg boasted that since my introduction of the term *conservative crack-up*, "conservative ideas [had] won under a Democratic president and [now] Republican politicians inexorably claimed majority party status in this country."[10] He dismissed warnings from John Micklethwait and Adrian Wooldridge in their then current book, *The Right Nation: Conservative Power in America*, that conservatism might become "too Southern, too greedy, too contradictory."[11]

Goldberg also dismissed the possibility that rivalries within the movement, namely between traditionalists and libertarians, might bring on fragmentation. For conservatives this rivalry was a long-standing concern. It was there in the movement's earliest days in the 1950s, as I shall relate in later chapters. I myself mentioned the rivalry in *The Conservative Crack-Up*. Such a potential for fragmentation has been a staple of conservative obituarists since the movement began. Goldberg was right to dismiss it. As I explained in *Crack-Up*, these rivalries never impeded conservative voter turnout any more than Liberal rivalries— say, between Big Labor and environmentalists—impeded Liberal voter turnout.

Unfortunately, toward the end of the Bush years, with scandals mounting, Republican fiscal laxness apparent, and Bush's leadership failing, the premonitions uttered by the authors of *The Right Nation* gained plausibility in political circles. By 2008 their warning that conservatism was catering to the rustics would become a fashionable critique of conservatism. After Senator John McCain tapped the evangelical governor of a rural state to be his running mate, their warning rose to the epistemological category of Washington "conventional wisdom," which for mainstream journalists and believing Democrats is Irrefutable Truth.

By then there had emerged a new set of conservative rivalries more disruptive than the earlier rivalry between libertarians and traditionalists. In the place of that rivalry, which was at least ostensibly about ideas, came rivalries among personalities, essentially about self-promotion. The arrival of the conservative personality was not an evolutionary breakthrough but a regression. Whereas in the past conservatism's most prominent voices had been intellectuals, by the 1990s the intellectuals had been replaced by personalities, that is to say entertaining controversialists, often astoundingly vulgar. Their rude arrival on the political scene was the unlovely consequence of America's intellectual decline. Sometimes the personality led a conservative organization—usually a single-issue organization, sometimes merely a radio audience. Often the personality became a megalomaniac, utterly insouciant to the wider interplay of ideas, policies, and organizations that normally comprise a political movement.

Starting at some point in the 1990s, one could earn a colossal income as a conservative personality, something that was unheard-of when the conservative movement was just getting started. "Every great cause begins as a movement becomes a business, and eventually degenerates into a racket," longshoreman philosopher Eric Hoffer writes in his 1951 classic, *The True Believer*.[12] Alas, by the presidency of Bush 43, blissful sectors of the conservative movement had become a racket. Conservative personalities were jetting to public appearances in private planes, hauling in huge honoraria, contributing gore and bombast to the public discourse. There was money to be made, celebrity to be courted, and not a great deal of intellect or learning required. A glum truth of recent decades is that standards of intellect in public life, particularly at the national level, have declined enormously. Where once there stood William F. Buckley Jr. at the rostrum now there stands Ann Coulter—her rival on the left might be James Carville, cackling, or Al Franken—now the Honorable Al Franken from the great state of Minnesota—simpering.

The conservatives' celebrity personalities lacked a serious grasp of the movement's founding principles and an intellectual's grasp of ideas and policies. The flimsiness of their achievement engendered jealousy among lesser conservative figures, creating defensiveness among the conservative celebs, many of whom eventually suffered, I assume, from the Impostor Syndrome, that is to say, the psychological syndrome in which the afflicted senses that he or she is, at the end of the day, a fraud. As I shall explain in melancholy detail, modern conservatism's evolution from intellectual minority status to its present popularity has been attended by increased insularity and jealousy among many conservative leaders. Insularity and pettiness are not assets in the pursuit of that great gregarious drama, democratic politics.

Not all conservative leaders suffer these faults—certainly the heads of the prodigiously productive think tanks have usually been immune to such pettiness. The demands placed on a person entrusted with finding the best policies for protecting American freedoms, values, and national security probably do not allow time for them to indulge petty impulses. Yet the movement's small fry—its minor writers, journalists, ephemeral pontificators, and many of its celebs—have often been pinched by a smallness that has set the movement back and encouraged intramural squabbling. To be sure, pettiness is a weakness shared by many intellectuals regardless of politics, but conservative intellectuals are more susceptible to petty competitiveness than Liberals. Anyone familiar with the Liberals' memoirs has beheld the spectacle of them heaving confetti at each other: Arthur M. Schlesinger Jr. in praise of John Kenneth Galbraith;[13] Noel Annan, the British academic, in praise of his whole generation of Liberals on both sides of the Atlantic.[14] Conservatives in the early years of the movement acted like this. Buckley was particularly given to such displays of geniality and magnanimity. Yet by the 1990s such grace was rare.

By the early twenty-first century, there was less bonhomie among conservatives than I had ever seen before. Often they simply ignored each other's work, a problem I first noted in the late 1980s when I was writing *The Conservative Crack-Up*. I mentioned the problem to Buckley back then, and his response inadvertently confirmed my observation. When I told him conservatives should take more interest in each other's work, he dismissed the suggestion as "boring." Pat Buchanan has noticed the conservatives' insularity, too, though in a grimmer context. In 2003 he wrote that conservatives "do not retrieve their wounded."[15] The line has reechoed among conservatives for years, but not much has changed.

There is a reason for this insularity among conservatives. They have been confined to the margins of political culture—not the margins of politics, where the voters rule, but of political culture, where the elites hold sway. American culture's honors and positions of authority have been successfully reserved for Liberals. No Pulitzer ever adorned Buckley's name despite his huge production of journalism and the large shadow he cast across the Republic, and there have been scores of other conservative leaders worthy of cultural honors, though few receive them. Thus, like university professors who fight for the paltry perks of academe, the conservatives snipe at each other. By the second Bush administration, the sniping increased, as did the neglect of each other. A dialogue among conservative intellectuals and scholars was as rare as dialogue between conservative thinkers and Liberals. The latter is somewhat understandable; the former is very disappointing.

When back in 2005 Goldberg foresaw only glad and glorious morns for conservatism, he did not take into account the ceaseless ebbs and flows of history that anyone intent on understanding politics must anticipate. Goldberg was about to have the sands shift under his feet. In his 2005 article he boasted, "The federal government is run by Republicans for as far as the eye can see."[16]

Then came the 2006 congressional elections. After the rout, with Democrats controlling the House of Representatives and ever so tenuously the Senate, Goldberg abruptly joined that lugubrious cadre that, as we have seen, has accompanied conservatism from the beginning. He became one of conservatism's obituarists. On January 13, 2008, under a *Washington Post* headline, "Cloudy Fortunes for Conservatism," the *National Review* contributing editor lamented, "Conservatism, quite simply, is a mess these days."[17] Mind you, Goldberg's descent from the smugness of 2005 to his despair in early 2008 is a turnaround that many political pundits experience at no cost to their colossal self-esteem or even to their credibility. One of my most deeply held insights into American politics is that what passes for Washington's conventional wisdom at any given time nowadays is usually stupendously in error. "The Liberals Are History," "Conservatism Is Dead," "Hillary Rodham's Democratic Nomination Is Inevitable," all those headlines have proved to be rubbish. Usually Washington's conventional wisdom is simply an amalgam of the hackneyed fatuities shared by popular pundits, who would rather get along with one another than be right. Contemporary political commentary in Washington is not so much an effort at empiricism as an effort at sociability.

The fashionable judgment repeated to the point of tedium after the 2008 election was that conservatism now faced years in the wilderness. If being wrong was a ticket to wilderness years, the pundits of 2008 should have been shuffling out there the night the polls closed. The conventional wisdom that they began to pass around early in the year was completely wrong. The "inevitability" that they spied in Senator Clinton's presidential nomination took no account of senior Democrats' obvious weariness of the Clinton scandals and awareness of the Clintons' propensity for self-inflicted wounds. Neither did the conventional wisdom pay heed to Hillary's dangerously high negative poll numbers or to the rising generation's desire for a Democratic nominee from its own generation. All this I had reported in my easily accessible 2007 book, *The Clinton Crack-Up*. The evidence was obvious. Still, for months prior to the Democratic primaries and despite Hillary's negative ratings always being at 40 percent or higher, the pundits pegged her as "the inevitable nominee." Brief weeks after the primaries began, she suffered an abrupt detumescence, becoming the second-rate candidate of an incompetently run, if lavishly funded, campaign, which now was broke and pitiable.

The Washington conventional wisdom regarding Senator Barack Obama has been equally nonsensical. He evolved from being a hopeless outsider to being the guarantor of "Hope!" and "Change!" Some change—weeks after his election, he was leading an incoming government of lobbyists, Washington insiders, Chicago cronies, and an unusually large number of tax cheats. His empty Senate seat became the locale for grafters and soon circumstantial evidence in the impeachment and eventual graft prosecution of his home-state governor and erstwhile ally. On the campaign trail, candidate Obama had inspired the pundits with his mantra that Washington's political system is "broken."[18] In the end he proved that it was indeed broken. The electorate, after rejecting the Clintons in the primaries, found itself by the 2009 inauguration saddled with what appeared to be a third Clinton administration. Hillary was designated secretary of state. President Clinton's former White House staffer Rahm Emanuel became Obama's chief of staff. Lesser Clintonistas had the president-elect surrounded.

The low standards of our pundits have been complemented by the low standards of our political leaders. Their mediocrity has been clearly observable since the first irregularities of the Clinton administration. The Bush administration that followed may have been more ethical and competent, but I doubt history will judge George W. Bush to be other than mediocre. What these two baby-boomer presidents have revealed is that the most ballyhooed generation since the Founding Fathers, that of the 1960s, is, at least in politics and in journalism, a colossal failure. Conservatism's obituarists bemoaning the decline of intellect within the conservative movement and remonstrating against the rise of Governor Sarah Palin and the rustics in the Republican Party would be more persuasive if they could point to high standards anywhere else on the political spectrum.

Dating at least from the early 1990s, mediocrity has been the norm in presidential politics, leavened occasionally by sheer weirdness. The era of mediocrity began when a scandal-tainted governor from Arkansas captured the Democratic presidential nomination from a field of has-beens. Revealed as a draft dodger, a marijuana user, and an inveterate liar (recall that Clinton was actually caught on tape coaching a former lover to lie to the press), his campaign should have been over. After such revelations, no previous presidential candidate in all the twentieth century would have won election. Not surprisingly, the presidency of such a rogue proved to be second-rate. The consensus among historians is that he may have been very clever, but his performance was very flawed. Clinton failed at every major initiative he attempted except his peace initiative in Northern Ireland. His failings were enormous, but his mediocrity is not unique.

Looking back on the 2000 presidential elections, one sees that neither party had a first-rate candidate in the running—though Steve Forbes, running for the Republican nomination might have made a fine president had he somehow kept the television cameras at a distance and suspended the journalists' obsession with charisma to win the election. Governor George W. Bush, despite coming from a politically seasoned family, had a weak résumé when he beat Vice President Al Gore, another mediocrity from a politically seasoned family. President Bush was a grave disappointment, but it is unthinkable that either Gore or the delusory senator John Kerry would have been an improvement. Both were the kind of fantasists we have come to expect from the prototypical Liberal presidential model, and Kerry was astounding. He actually ran in 2004 claiming to be a Vietnam hero despite the existence of TV footage showing him before Congress, protesting the Vietnam War. There he testified to knowing that his comrades in arms had "personally raped, cut off ears, cut off heads, taped wires from portable telephones to human genitals and turned up the power, cut off limbs, blown up bodies, randomly shot at civilians, razed villages in fashion reminiscent of Genghis Khan . . ."[19] Could anyone expect to be elected president with that skeleton in the closet?

The field of contenders in 2008 was equally bleak, ultimately pitting a novice against a maverick. Whoever won in 2008, the string of presidential mediocrities was bound to continue. Had Senator John McCain been elected, he probably would have been a better president than his opponent, but he would undoubtedly have been wrangling with conservatives and even moderates for all of his time in office. As for Senator McCain's Democratic opponent, it is now clear that Senator Barack Obama is the most ill-prepared man to become president since Abraham Lincoln's abrupt successor, Andrew Johnson, who at least had the alibi of being a drunkard.

Lower down on the 2008 ticket, both Sarah Palin and the delightful Senator Joe Biden were obvious mediocrities, though Biden has the distinction of being the more experienced mediocrity, with almost four decades of unimpressive service to his country to boast of. Before she can match Biden's record, Palin has to achieve decades of middling service, and it is doubtful she can ever equal his clownishness. Her nomination at the Republican National Convention was supposedly a sign of conservatism's dire straits and the rise of the rustics. Yet in her campaign against Biden, the Delaware blabbermouth far surpassed her in gaffs both in number and in basic human stupidity.

Interviewed by CBS's Katie Couric early in the campaign, Biden claimed that Franklin Roosevelt was president during the 1929 crash of the stock market and that Roosevelt immediately "got on television" to address the American people.[20] Incidentally, when Biden uttered this preposterosity, Couric's face betrayed no hint that she recognized that Herbert Hoover was president in 1929 and that there was no national television audience in existence—again journalistic mediocrity. Biden's gaffs continued. Despite having been ignominiously forced from the 1988 Democratic presidential primaries for plagiarizing British Labour Party leader Neil Kinnock's recollections of life in

Welsh coal mines, Biden BS'd an audience of Virginia coal miners that when he was young, he had been "a hard coal miner"—a total fabrication.[21] About this time he was caught lying (repeatedly!) about his helicopter having been forced down by enemy fire along the Afghanistan-Pakistan border. Ultimately, the press reported that inclement weather was the cause.[22]

More seriously, during a debate with Palin, Biden erroneously claimed that the United States "drove Hezbollah out of Lebanon."[23] Nothing of the kind had happened. More amusingly, he declared, "The number one job facing the middle class . . . happens to be as Barack says, a three-letter word, jobs. J-O-B-S, jobs."[24] The gaffable candidate made all these misstatements within a four-week period in early autumn, beginning with some memorable advice to a journalist covering him. Tapping the reporter on the chest (I assume the journalist was a male), Biden advised, "You need to work on your pecs."[25] Despite all this, the conventional wisdom was that Palin was inexperienced, not that Biden was a buffoon. Again, her nomination was supposedly a reflection of conservatism's intellectual decline.

Truth be known, intellectual decline is everywhere within America's national political leadership. According to Washington's conventional wisdom, the explanation is that our best citizens stay out of politics rather than suffer the press's intrusions into their private lives, intrusions that allegedly began with Watergate and became more egregious during the Clinton scandals. This explanation is plausible, though before lamenting the politicians' ransacked privacy, note that it is frequently the politicians themselves who invite the press into their private lives. The modern presidential candidate is a veritable exhibitionist. With the ongoing evolution of the prototypical Liberal presidential model, candidates tell us about their alcoholic parents (Clinton), spouses' private addictions (Dukakis), the embarrassment of being a fat boy in the schoolyard (Clinton, again), and much more. At the 1992 and 1996 Democratic National Conventions, Vice President Gore exploited his son's automobile accident and then his sister's death from lung cancer.[26]

There is, however, a deeper explanation for the mediocrity of our political leadership than the potential candidates' lost privacy. The truth is that only a troubled person would aspire to political leadership today. No normal person would embark on the 24/7 campaign schedule that is required—often for years—of a successful presidential nominee. That is the kind of commitment that could only be made by a narcissist, an egomaniac, or some other variant of a social misfit. The first candidate to make it was Governor Jimmy Carter. I rest my case. The most recent candidate to make this monstrous commitment has been Senator Obama, who, though only in the Senate for a few weeks, dispatched aides to Iowa to begin what would be his three-year quest for the presidential nomination. He is a marathon exhibitionist. During his first year in office, he continued to campaign. For that matter, during Bill Clinton's retirement he, too, has continued to campaign, though for what office, it remains unclear.

Equally relevant to the mediocrity of our political leadership is the tremendous decline of intellect in public life. I referred to it earlier in mentioning the rivalries of the conservative personalities. The decline has been going on for a generation, perhaps more. I cannot think of a truly thoughtful person who has had a shot at becoming president since the late 1980s. I referred admiringly to Steve Forbes earlier, but in hindsight his campaigns were hopeless.

The only presidential candidates acclaimed for their intellects over the past two decades have been Clinton and Obama, neither of whom has ever produced anything of scholarly merit, not even a pamphlet. Clinton never finished his degree at Oxford and has never written anything noteworthy for anything other than bombast and balderdash. His vast bouillabaisse of a presidential memoir is dreadful, replete with obvious falsehoods, many of which had previously been exposed when he first uttered them during his presidency. For the most part, the book was written by a team of collaborators, who must have had a difficult time keeping up with their globe-trotting subject matter. The only writing Clinton *indisputably* contributed to the project involves personal revelations, at times touching but usually just plain weird.

Obama, during his three years in the Senate, never authored an important bill. As an Illinois senator he voted "present" 129 times. He was president of the *Harvard Law Review*, but that is basically a political achievement (which incidentally, he won with the support of the *Review*'s conservatives). While at Harvard he never wrote anything of any intellectual distinction. In fact, at the *Harvard Law Review* he never published anything under his name. Neither did he publish anything under his name while at the University of Chicago Law School. His memoir, *Dreams from My Father*, has fleeting moments of eloquence, an eloquence that Obama has never achieved anywhere else. He is to this day embarrassingly dependent on teleprompters. If down the road it is proved that his memoir was actually written by someone else, as has now been suggested by many,[27] I shall not be any more surprised than I was when it was proved that JFK's *Profiles in Courage* was written by his aide, Ted Sorensen, who got no credit for the book's Pulitzer Prize.

Given the intellectual barrenness of our political landscape, the complaint that the conservative movement had thrown in with the rustics by the end of the Bush years rings hollow. According to variations of the charge, the conservative movement was "out of ideas," "intellectually exhausted," and headed for the wilderness. The final proof of our demise was supposedly McCain's choice of Palin as his running mate. During the 2008 election and immediately thereafter, I occasionally referred to her as the "pulchritudinous governor of Alaska." It was one joke that both Liberals and conservatives agreed on—not funny. Well, mark that down as evidence that politics is no longer the domain of the civilized.

The vexed reaction to Palin was almost comic. She was nowhere near the bungler that Biden was. But neither was she likely to become president of the United States, as some conservatives contended. She was simply a modestly gifted political newcomer who dazzled before the cameras and took positions that the so-called sophisticates loathed. Charles Krauthammer had it just right in his wrap-up of the election when he wrote that her candidacy provoked a "sideshow psychodrama of feminist rage and elite loathing that had little to do with politics and everything to do with cultural prejudices, resentments, and affectations."[28]

PINCHED
BY CRABS

Among the Benedict Arnolds,
Backstabbers, Bruti, and Bums

The reaction to Governor Sarah Palin and her rustics, the evangelical and middle-American enthusiasts who were wowed by her, revealed a new set of conservative rivalries that differed from those among conservative personalities. The new rivalries were to some degree generational. What they revealed was that some by now middle-aged conservatives took American conservatism for granted. They did not realize how difficult it had been for earlier generations of conservatives to create the organizations—the think tanks, the magazines, the political and advocacy groups—that were founded in the conservative movement's formative years and flourished through the last two decades of the twentieth century. Yet by 2008 those organizations were secure even if their conservative critics were not. The organizations were rooted in the 40 percent or so of the American people who considered themselves conservative. They were not dependent on the popularity of the pulchritudinous Governor Palin.

This new rivalry that was on display in the aftermath of the 2008 Republican defeat was begun by younger conservatives doing what ambitious conservatives occasionally have done before: advancing themselves at the expense of fellow conservatives, in this case the curvaceous Sarah, those smitten by her, and those stodgy movement conservatives who peer through the *Kultursmog* and still perceive the fundamental reality of American politics. To wit, it is the ideas and principles of American conservatism that fetch the American majority. It is the ideas and excesses of Liberalism that repel the American majority. Hence, at the end of 2009, Gallup could report that conservatism was twice as popular among Americans as Liberalism. In fact, Gallup found more Americans identifying with the designation "conservative" than with "moderate."[1] And one other point: conservatism's base, though turbulent, is not nearly as unsteady as Liberalism's.

Ross Douthat was the youngest soi-disant conservative grinding an ax against the conservative movement that had made his career possible—and, of course, against Palin. He reflected the superficiality of the young conservative grumblers soon after the 2008 election, when he reviewed William F. Buckley Jr.'s posthumously published book, *The Reagan I Knew*. Palin was still a boil on the brains of conservatism's critics, Douthat's included. From his ensuing irritable discourse, it became clear that Douthat's knowledge of the conservative movement was as superficial as his anxiety about Palin was faked. Surely he knew that she was not going to be taking over the Republican Party.

Reviewing Buckley in the *New York Times Book Review*, Douthat wrote that during the 2008 presidential election, "populism's corrosive influence on the conservative mind—or the conservative mind's cynical manipulation of populism—was cited in briefs against Sarah Palin, against the record of George W. Bush and against the entire run of conservative governance going back to Richard Nixon," which, of course, does not make those briefs true or authoritative. The "briefs" might have been the work of ignoramuses or of Liberal partisans. Contrary to Douthat's assumption, their allegations do not make conservatives guilty of populism or of demagoguery, which is really what is being insinuated here.

Douthat continued: "A populist spirit—the same spirit that gave us talk radio, Fox News and 'drill, baby, drill'—has hung over post-war conservatism from its inception,"[2] which is nonsense. Nixon never claimed to be a member of the conservative movement, and he never was. Populism had no place in the conservative movement, which was in its early days criticized for being not populist but elitist and a tool of the rich. More recently it has been charged with being middle class and middlebrow. Growing from a small group of intellectuals in the late 1940s into a popular political movement capable of capturing government and changing the course of history, conservatism has had little to do with populism. The term was coined at the end of the nineteenth century for a mongrel political movement that mixed agrarianism with labor in a brief alliance rooted in sectionalism, nativism, and racism. It did not last.

Used as Douthat has, "populism" is a vulgar mis-
nomer employed by ignorant journalists with the same
airy disregard for the meaning of words that they display
when they call advocates of the Iraq War "neoconservatives."
Neoconservatism has a specific meaning in American political history, dating from the late 1960s, as we shall see in
later chapters. A more accurate designation for the Iraq
War's supporters would be "hawks," the term used for
supporters of controversial wars in the past, for instance,
the Vietnam War. Such terminological slovenliness is but
another example of the political landscape's intellectual
barrenness.

As for Palin, she is not a populist but an advocate of
traditional family values, a person of faith—in this case
evangelical Christianity—and an otherwise mundane
Republican. She represents that element in the American
electorate that New Dealers might have called "the common man." There is nothing unusual or inappropriate or
populist about politicians—conservative or otherwise—
trying to win an election by courting the common man.
Neither is it a sign of intellectual exhaustion. Obama was
pretty much doing the same in choosing Biden as his running mate.

The conservative movement was founded on ideas that
have nothing to do with populism. It is an intellectual tradition tracing back through the Founding Fathers to eighteenth-
century British statesman and philosopher Edmund Burke,
and even beyond Burke to Aristotle. In the modern context,
conservatism derives its intellectual sustenance from the

Federalist Papers, James Madison's *Notes of Debates in the Federal Convention of 1787*, the Constitution, and the Declaration of Independence. Russell Kirk, one of the founders of modern conservatism, believed our Constitution to be one of the wisest conservative documents ever drawn up. Frank Meyer, another of the movement's founders, admired the Constitution for its "restriction of government to its proper functions: within government, tension and balance between local and central power; within the Federal Government, tension and balance between the coordinate branches."[3] Based on such documents and defended by the likes of Kirk and Meyer, the conservative movement hardly qualifies as populist.

Douthat is a minor figure in what by the 2008 election could be considered as another subgroup of conservatives then fragmenting from the original conservative movement. I call them the Reformed Conservatives (RCs). Whether they actually had a twelve-step program to help them along, I cannot say. I am not even sure they will be around for long. The drastic slippage of Democrats in the polls in 2009 and their electoral reversals in that off-year election completely discredited the RCs' prophesies of conservative demise. From autumn 2008 to autumn 2009, Democrats saw their twelve-point lead over Republicans in the Gallup generic poll collapse, leaving the Republicans with a four-point lead over the Democrats (48 percent to 44 percent).[4] Interestingly, in 1994, the year of the Republicans' historic takeover of Congress, the Republicans never eclipsed the Democrats until March of that year, and that was only by one point.

The RCs' criticism of conservatives pleases Liberals, but it is shallow and ill informed. It has not fetched many conservatives or even moderates. The RCs have usually adopted the aforementioned tactic of ingratiating themselves with the mainstream Liberal media by finding fault with conservatism. The tactic worked for Douthat, who replaced the vastly more accomplished and knowledgeable William Kristol—founder and editor of the *Weekly Standard*—as a columnist at the *New York Times*. Kristol's credentials as a movement conservative go back to the late 1960s, when as a boy he was more of a conservative than his distinguished father, Irving Kristol, who then was a conventional Liberal. In 1968 Irving endorsed the presidential candidacy of Senator Hubert Humphrey, a staunch Liberal and member in good standing of the Liberal Americans for Democratic Action (ADA). Eventually, as Liberalism radicalized, Irving led some Liberals, who were disaffected by this radicalism, into the conservative movement under the banner "neoconservative." In the process he was dubbed the "Godfather of Neoconservatism" in *Esquire* magazine,[5] but his son got to conservatism first.

At the *Times* Douthat has positioned himself above the old Liberal-versus-conservative fray, but not very convincingly. On important matters he is usually supportive of his Liberal patrons. A particularly treacherous example of this dissembling took place during the Senate hearings on the Supreme Court nomination of Judge Sonia Sotomayor. In his *Times* column Douthat depicted Senator Jeff Sessions of Alabama, a solid and respectable movement conservative, thus: "Her chief Republican interlocutor, Jeff Sessions of Alabama, even has a history of racially charged remarks."[6] Douthat did not bother to adduce the evidence of Sessions's "racially charged remarks," but in the online version of the column, Douthat did link the passage to an eleven-week-old article in the online magazine *Politico*.[7] There *Politico* reported that twenty-three years before, during Sessions's own brutally partisan Senate hearings for a seat on the federal bench, Sessions was accused of favoring the Ku Klux Klan and calumniating the National Association for the Advancement of Colored People (NAACP) as "un-American" and "communist-inspired."

Reviewing the accusations, I found that both were obvious distortions, apparent to anyone who might bother to investigate such a serious charge. The first stemmed from an amusing joke Sessions made to friends when he wisecracked that he thought the Klansmen "okay" until he heard that some were "pot smokers." The NAACP remark was a private expression of concern for the organization's reputation voiced by Sessions, who was at the time a federal prosecutor. He told two black colleagues, one of whom became a disgruntled employee, that the NAACP's attacks on the Reagan administration's foreign policy toward the Sandinistas might be *construed* as "un-American" and "communist-inspired." He never defamed the organization. Both charges against him were unjustified. Most important, over the next twenty-three years, the senator from Alabama's record was unblemished by any hint of bigotry or any other unwholesome blemish aside from being the solid conservative that Douthat claims somehow to be. Douthat is not only shallow; he is deceitful.

The most well-known RCs have been the two Davids: David Brooks and David Frum. They compose what I like to call the Davidian Branch of Reformed Conservatism. Their stated goal is to modernize Ronald Reagan's conservatism for the twenty-first century, presumably without the conflagration earlier Davidians provoked. The two Davids were of about the same age in 2008, their late forties. Both got their starts in the conservative movement, Brooks at the *National Review*, from which he proceeded to the *Washington Times,* the *Wall Street Journal,* and the *Weekly Standard*; Frum from the *Wall Street Journal* to the *Weekly Standard*, to the *National Review*, and finally his own Web site, presumptuously named NewMajority.com. He has had stops along the way at conservative think tanks, namely, the Manhattan Institute and the American Enterprise Institute, where he has long maintained an office. He also had stints as a columnist at *Forbes* and at the *American Spectator*, where he did a fine column on public policy, though our waggish editorial director, Wladyslaw Pleszczynski, used to mock the fussiness that often characterizes Frum's work by calling him "Frump."

Evolutionists can point to Frum's intellectual development as a validation of Charles Darwin's theory of evolution and natural selection. In his 1994 book, *Dead Right,* Frum inveighed against the Reagan administration's failure to advance what he properly deemed a leading desideratum of the conservative movement, paring back big government. Later Frum served as a presidential speechwriter in the George W. Bush administration, where he encouraged the false claim that he had authored the administration's phrase "axis of evil." Upon being exposed, he settled for being identified as a writer who had *assisted* in creating the phrase, which somehow does not ring true. Even in a government bureaucracy, how many writers are needed to create a three-word phrase? At any rate, he left the Bush White House abruptly to write *The Right Man: The Surprise Presidency of George W. Bush*, in which he proclaimed the forty-third president "nothing short of superb."[8] Over the next few years, as the intellectual climate changed, Frum underwent the necessary mutations required by natural selection and wrote *Comeback: Conservatism That Can Win Again*, wherein he argued that if conservatism is to survive, it must favor government expansion, reject tax reform, and deemphasize social issues. Frum's estimate of Bush changed, too, for by the time he wrote *Comeback*, he believed that Bush "led his party to the brink of disaster."[9] Frum, like his Davidian colleague, Brooks, is mainly a sedentary creature, yet both are forever tendering politicians advice on tactics and strategies. Occasionally it has seemed that they have aspired to being Karl Rove or perhaps even the candidate himself. If Darwin were alive in the last years of the Bush administration, doubtless he would have taken Frum home and put him in a jar.

Both Davidians have advocated that conservatives engage in the "battle of ideas," though they were not themselves very bellicose. Noting that population changes were increasing the ratios of Latinos and socially Liberal young people in the country, Frum advised conservatives to adapt their policies accordingly. Brooks shared this policy of accommodation and momentarily became the most notorious RC of all by calling Palin "a cancer to the Republicans Party."[10] This happened while he was being interviewed by the *Atlantic* magazine over French cuisine at Le Cirque in Manhattan. Brooks was not talking about cancer in a mild form. He called Palin "a fatal cancer."

Conservatism's Davidians claimed to fear that conservatives were losing touch with the intelligentsia, by which they meant the middlebrow, not the highbrow, intelligentsia. After all, conservatives rarely had a chance with the highbrows, except for that period in the late 1960s and early 1970s when Irving Kristol's Liberal intellectuals became neoconservatives. The Davidians seemed to have in mind urban and suburban sophisticates: readers of the *New York Times*, grim practitioners of yoga and Pilates, people at home with fears about global cooling in the 1970s, global warming since the 1990s, and the general condition of the globe 24/7. Truth be known, on the subject of intellectuals, Frum has been rather mysterious. He has fretted that conservative intellectuals have been losing touch with America, but in nothing he has written has it been clear that he ever reads conservative intellectuals, at least none still living.

After the 2008 election, Brooks wrote a column predicting that conservatives (he called them the "Traditionalists") were going to tighten their hold on the weakened

Republican Party and ensure years of Republican defeats.[11] Part of the prediction was sound. Conservatives did tighten their hold on the party, but, as we have seen, Brooks's prophesied defeats were actually victories and a rising Republican popularity, especially among independents who by autumn 2009 favored Republicans over Democrats by 22 percent according to the Gallup Poll.[12] This is not to say that conservatism does not have its difficulties. We have already mentioned some: for instance, the conservative's comparatively weak political libido as against that of the Liberal, whose political libido is often that of a sex offender. Then again the fractious rivalries among conservatives are debilitating, and there is a tendency for conservatives to promote one issue at the expense of a full agenda: the proponent of military readiness who ignores economics, the supply-sider who is insouciant to culture. Yet over the years the conservatives (the Traditionalists, to Brooks) have been very competitive against the once-dominant Liberals. Before predicting years of Republican defeats, the Davidians and anyone else curious about the future of American politics might have contemplated the unstable state of Liberalism.

What the conservative movement's eager obituarists always have failed to take into account is the volatile nature of conservatism's adversary, Liberalism. The critics who consigned conservatism to the wilderness in 2008 should have taken a look at the ideological fanatics who were coming into Washington with the novice Barack Obama, himself a community organizer with a head full of slogans from the late Saul Alinsky. Conservatives have suffered through wilderness years in the past. Every time they have emerged stronger, in part because many Americans agree with them, in part because since the 1960s, Liberalism has been in a whirl.

Liberalism's core values keep changing, usually radicalizing even as its conceits remain petrified in time, lost in reveries of yesteryear's Deals and Frontiers and presidents so idolized that we need only mention their initials, FDR, JFK, LBJ. No wait! Delete that last one. That Society of his has never made it into the Liberal fantasia. For one thing, its excesses marked the beginning of the conservatives' dominance of presidential politics.

The Liberals' juggling of their core values began back in the 1960s. Over the past generation they have valued freedom and civil liberties in one instance, say, during the Church Committees' investigation of the FBI and the CIA, or later during George W. Bush's domestic surveillance of terrorists. In other instances, they have championed the antithesis, government control; say, their environmental rulings against property owners, their social engineering projects, their exorbitant taxation, and increased government regulation of commerce. Occasionally they are simply schizophrenic, stressing personal freedom *and* government control simultaneously, say, in the Obama administration's drive to computerize Americans' medical records.

Through the decades, there has only been one Liberal principle that the Liberals have agreed on without fluctuation. That is their solemn belief that it is fundamental to the progress of our nation that Liberals disturb the peace. Liberal folklore abounds with Disturbers of the Peace who become mythic figures until one of their disturbing qualities falls out of ever-changing Liberal fashion: H. L. Mencken, dropped because of his racial and ethnic prejudices; Mark Twain, dropped because of excessive use of the N-Word in his fiction; Justice William O. Douglas, dropped when perceived to be a misogynist; Clarence Darrow, dropped for excessive cigarette smoking. Disturbing the peace is the Liberals' founding principle, predating even the New Deal. It is their one principle that never changes. Rather amusingly, it is codified a misdemeanor in most civilized countries. In the Arab world it is probably a felony. Liberalism is the world's only nontotalitarian political movement founded on a petty crime.

Since the Reagan presidency, Liberalism has endured more years of decline than ascendancy. Listening to the sweeping rhetoric of President Obama and witnessing the shifting emphases in his brief tenure, I think we can conclude that Liberalism is again in one of its periods of schizophrenia. An epic battle between Liberalism and conservatism is taking place, and the conservatives have far more strength today in numbers, in institutions, and in ideas than they did in any of the earlier battles, for instance, the historic upheavals of the 1960s and the 1930s—though the 1930s conservatives differed markedly from today's more flexible and intellectual conservatives. Contrary to the Davidians, the conservatives will be making this a battle of ideas and principles.

I first diagnosed Liberals' unstable condition in the early 1980s, in my book *The Liberal Crack-Up*. At the time, the book did not get much attention from Liberals, even from Liberal scholars, despite the evidence amassed and a profusion of scholarly citations. Now it is gratifying to see that the book's insights are being recognized by historians and political scientists who understand that Liberalism's unstable values have led to its own fragmentation and to an extremism that has alienated ordinary Americans to the point that during national elections Liberalism is often euphemized as the *L*-Word."

Sean Wilentz, the distinguished Princeton University historian, notes Liberalism's worsening condition in his revisionist study, *The Age of Reagan: A History, 1974–2008*. "The decline of the old party mechanisms," he writes of the late 1970s, "had fragmented the Democrats into dozens of disconnected interest groups."[13] A decade later, the Liberals' fragmentation had become even more visible. Wilentz writes, "Plagued by divisions of race, ideology, and political temperament that dated back to the late 1960s; unable to unite around a coherent set of attitudes, let alone ideas about foreign policy and the military or domestic issues; beholden to a disparate collection of special constituencies and interest groups, each with its own agenda, the quarrelsome Democrats made the fractured Republican Party look like a juggernaut."[14]

In the aftermath of the Democrats' 2008 victory, it was apparently impossible for RCs and the conventional journalists to recall that Republican Party "juggernaut." Mark that down as another example of the conventional wisdom's ability to claim infallibility even as it slips on the banana peel of error and suffers continued memory loss. The fact is that just two or three years before the 2008 obituaries were being written for conservatism, similarly pessimistic reports were being filed for the Liberal Democrats.

Our volatile politics have unsettled the conventional wisdom. From the Republicans' 2000 victory until their 2006 congressional setback, it was the Democrats who were certified as an endangered species within the conventional wisdom. Consider a sampling from the conventional wisdom of 2000: "The Republicans now control the White House," CBS News reported on December 14, 2000, "the Senate (with Vice President-elect Cheney soon to be the tie-breaking vote) and the House of Representatives, and they have a majority on the U.S. Supreme Court."[15] The CBS report continued, "Here's the reality for Democrats, whether they choose to accept it or not: This is now, in many important ways, a Republican country, in terms of power . . . Gore found out the hard way just how Republican the country as a whole has turned over the past quarter century."[16] As we have seen, the country became even more Republican two years later, when George W. Bush became the first president since FDR to increase his margins in his first congressional elections.[17]

By 2004 the Democrats' prospects, as deposited in the conventional wisdom, were even more gruesome, and Democratic leaders shared the gloom. The *New York Times* reported that "Democrats said President Bush's defeat of

Senator John Kerry by three million votes had left the party facing its most difficult time in at least 20 years."[18] Especially worrying to these Democrats was "the absence of any compelling Democratic leader prepared to steer the party back to power or carry its banner in 2008."[19] This, despite the first nationwide apparition of the Prophet Obama brief months before at the 2004 Democratic National Convention! *USA Today* confirmed the grim conventional wisdom. It reported that the 2004 election "extended the Republican Party's decade-long majority in the House of Representatives and its two-year majority in the Senate. It has been 71 years since Democrats were so shut out of power for so long in Washington. Though the margin of defeat was narrow in the contest for the presidency and in many congressional races, the scope of the party's losses left many Democrats reeling."[20]

As the Democrats reeled, they had to endure the same kind of know-it-all lectures that the Republicans would endure from their Davidians in the very next presidential election. A comparison of the two sets of lectures reveals an astonishing finding, one unobserved by any previous student of recent American politics before me—and now you. My Pulitzer Prize is within reach! I hope you will attend the ceremony.

The same issues perceived in 2004 by the Democrats' know-it-all lecturers as the Republicans' silver bullets were perceived four years later by the Republicans' know-it-all lecturers as hopeless Republican vulnerabilities. In 2004 the "social issues" that eventually were to be identified by the

Davidians and the RCs as Sarah Palin's folly were the despair of such defeatists as former congressman Dick Gephardt, who spoke for them all when he told *USA Today*, "Democrats have to find a way to counter the Republicans' appeal to voters opposed to gay marriage, gun control, and abortion."[21] Or consider what in 2008 David Frum considered the Republicans' shrinking political base, bereft of Latinos and hip urban sophisticates. A mere four years before, Senator Evan Bayh, the Indiana Democrat then being touted as a likely 2008 presidential prospect, fretted to the *New York Times* that "we need to be a party that stands for more than the sum of our resentments. In the heartland, where I come from, there are doubts. Too often we're caricatured as a bicoastal cultural elite that is condescending at best and contemptuous at worst to the values that Americans hold in their daily lives."[22]

So the know-it-alls in both parties are not as knowledgeable as they presume to be. And the condition of Liberalism and conservatism oscillates. Somehow, whether "cracked-up" or in Wilentz's terms, "fragmented," both conservatism and Liberalism wobble on. What remain constant are the faulty memory and the unreliable perceptions of the conventional wisdom. Let me repeat what I said in the last chapter. The conventional wisdom is almost always wrong. There is, we are told, long-term memory and short-term memory. The conventional wisdom seems to have neither.

What it does have is a hankering for bad news, particularly about conservatives. Hence, after the 2008 election conservatives endured all the dark murmurings about their impending wilderness years. There was an even grimmer forecast. Sam Tanenhaus, the editor of the *New York Times Book Review*, filed the lengthiest conservative obituary on record, first as an essay in the *New Republic*, later as a book. Both spoke of the Conservative movement being "dead."[23]

Faced with death or the wilderness years, I opted for the great outdoors. Right after the election, at the *American Spectator*'s Robert L. Bartley Dinner, annually given for our writers and supporters, I urged that we had best prepare for the wilderness. To help my friends survive, my staff distributed four hundred copies of the L. L. Bean catalog. Admittedly, the L. L. Bean company was suspicious when the *Spectator* ordered them for an annual dinner having more to do with politics than with fishing, hiking, or bird-watching.

The famous catalog features sportswear and outdoor accoutrements for every circumstance. Winston Churchill, during his wilderness years, was comforted by cases of Pol Roger and fistfuls of Havanas. Unfortunately, nowadays champagne is very pricey and smoking is *malum prohibitum* almost everywhere. Even in the great outdoors, a lit cigar could be highly controversial. So I urged my friends to settle for the offerings made available in the Bean catalog. Properly attired, we might not find the wilderness so bad. Sure, there would be poison ivy and wolves, clouds of mosquitoes and grimfaced members of the World Wildlife Federation stomping around on the mountain laurel, but there would be many instances of natural beauty. Once in the wilderness, I planned to pitch my tent close to that of the comely Governor Palin. She is very cute and can handle a shootin' iron. Moreover I heard tell that she has an excellent recipe for sautéed elk and would probably drive out in her Hummer. That hardy vehicle might prove useful. Assuming that the governing Liberals were about to perform as recklessly as in the past, we conservatives would probably be clearing out of the wilds in a hurry and heading back to the campaign trail. As it turned out, conservatism's wilderness years only lasted a few months, and I never did get an opportunity to taste Palin's sautéed elk.

What differs between the cracked-up condition of conservatism and what Wilentz calls the "fragmented" condition of Liberalism is that the conservatives have suffered their ideological divisions since the movement began and gained political power nonetheless—which is not to say that during the presidency of George W. Bush there were no portentous developments. While cast in the role of the country's dominant party, the Republican Party suffered a dreadful wasting away of its conservative values. Old-fashioned corruption did indeed steal into the GOP, a party that had been relatively free of corruption in modern times. Here I am not talking about that relatively new conception of corruption, to wit, the indictment of White House officials because of policy disagreements, as happened, for instance, with the Iran-Contra imbroglio. I am talking about the corruption of the good old days, of Tammany Hall, of ABSCAM, and of commonplace payoffs on the Hill in the 1980s. I am talking about the intrigues of the likes of Jack

Abramoff, Congressman Bob Ney, and Congressman Randy "Duke" Cunningham.

What is more, there were less perceptible problems confronting the conservatives as the Bush years lengthened. By 2008 there was an apparent exhaustion among the ranks. Sadder still, a whole generation of conservative leaders, political and intellectual, passed away. They were the remaining leaders who founded or shaped the modern conservative movement. Milton Friedman, Jesse Helms, Jack Kemp, Jeane Kirkpatrick, Paul Weyrich, they and so many others . . . all gone. Even the perennial *enfant terrible*, William F. Buckley Jr., was gone—while we faced 2010 and the conservatives' road to recovery.

3

ASCENDED AND STALLED

Adrift on the Zephyrs and Gusts
of the Zeitgeist

A memorial service for the third most famous of the conservative movement's historic figures could not have been held anyplace else but in a Roman Catholic cathedral, the country's most glorious Roman Catholic cathedral, St. Patrick's, right across the street from Rockefeller Center. There, behind the great gothic church's 20,000-pound bronze doors and underneath its 330-foot spires, a diverse crowd of 2,200 mourners had gathered to honor William F. Buckley, Jr. The deceased was devoutly Catholic, from which, as he told David Frost in a 1996 interview, all his other commitments followed.[1]

Barry Goldwater and Ronald Reagan did the political work to bring the movement to political dominance, but Bill was preeminent among those who did the intellectual work. Other intellectuals did work that was more scholarly and intellectually consequential, most notably Milton Friedman; but Bill was the intellectual who popularized the movement, on campus, in the media, and on television. What is more, he did so with an urbanity that the Liberals were not expecting. Perhaps they were looking for a rasping, snorting Senator Joe McCarthy that they could understand, or a stodgy Senator Robert A. Taft. Instead, they were sideswiped by Bill's awesome mix of culture, intellect, and wit. "Wasn't it remarkable," conservative New York editor Adam Bellow remarked at Bill's death, "how one man was able to infuse an entire movement with his own high intellectual standards and his tone of unfailing civility."[2] The civility theme became very popular among eulogists after Bill died on February 27, 2008, but those of us who are familiar with Bill's early years and actually witnessed the first televised debates on his public television show, *Firing Line*, knew the civility came later. In the first phases of Bill's career, he was a fierce polemicist and debater, occasionally showing no civility at all. When roused, he could strike like a viper. Yet, as Bellow said, Bill did "infuse an entire movement" with many of his virtues, one of which was apparent here at St. Patrick's. He was a devout, at times almost mystical, Catholic. Eventually, many around him converted. It was a danger one hazarded in being with him. Early twenty-first-century atheists might call it collateral damage.

I recall a story he told me one summer evening in 1979 after the two of us watched Jimmy Carter wander through what came to be known as Jimmy's "malaise speech," one of his memorable missteps toward his 1980 defeat. Slouched on a couch in the television room of his Victorian country house in Stamford, Connecticut, surrounded by red enameled walls—all the interior walls were red—Bill turned to the topic of faith and devotion to the Holy Eucharist. Jimmy was forgotten. Bill spoke in awe of a nun once living in a nearby abbey who displayed what he believed was exemplary piety while kneeling at the altar rail to receive Communion. A flu bug was running through her community, and a stricken nun kneeling next to her regurgitated the wafer after the priest had placed it in her mouth. The first nun immediately leaned over and lifted the wafer with her tongue lest it lie in the vomit. That was the kind of faith Bill hoped he had. For all I know he did. He was a frequent communicant, totally accepting the tenets of his church. He prayed the rosary. As a boy in the large Catholic family of his father, an oil man, he and his sister Trish would secretly baptize houseguests without their knowledge, much less consent. He had heard such baptisms worked. Perhaps that explains the later conversions among so many of his associates.

On this rainy April day, a full house had packed St. Patrick's to attend what turned out to be a most solemn and ornate requiem mass. The amalgamation of high seriousness with the highly dramatic was a Buckley trademark. The mourners faced eighteen priests standing like colorful statues on the faraway altar. The altar rail was marked off and perfumed by Easter lilies. Very little light shone through the immense stained glass windows on this grey day, but the cathedral's great organ groaned and fluted old hymns to raise our spirits and Adagio in A Minor by Bill's favorite composer, J. S. Bach, whom he delighted in torturing on his harpsichord.

Then a plump pastor got the proceedings under way with a blessing. As some audience members craned their necks to glimpse the latest famous figure to enter the gothic cavern, the thought occurred to some of us who had been with the conservative movement since the 1960s that the movement had come a long way from the days when, as the joke had it, the whole movement might fit into a Manhattan phone booth.

Senator Joe Lieberman, the Democrats' recent vice presidential candidate, arrived late, but it was gracious of him to be there. Bill had supported his senatorial race in 1988 over the Republican maverick Lowell Weicker.[3] Senator George McGovern, a friend of Bill's late in life despite political differences, was there too. Vice President Dick Cheney had wanted to attend, but the security arrangements made his presence prohibitive. Tom Wolfe looked splendid in white. I am sure I spotted Mike Wallace, the ageless CBS News correspondent emeritus who, at age ninety-one, might well be too old to die. He would often be at Bill's table at Bill's many fetes. I was always tempted to tease him about run-ins we had had—for instance, the time he deviously called me requesting that the *American Spectator* leak to his *60 Minutes* program advance copies of our forthcoming Clinton exposes. "We'll give you proper acknowledgment, Bob. Great publicity."

Sure, Mike.

After Wolfe and Wallace came Charlie Rose and Bill's skiing buddy, the legendary playboy and journalist, Taki Theodoracopulos. I was struck by how many TV journalists were there from a younger generation, men like Chris Matthews, who did not know Bill very well but wanted to be in St. Patrick's that morning. Bill, at the end of his life, was something more than one of modern conservatism's most famous faces. He was an icon.

From the mid-1960s to at least the end of the 1980s, Bill had been the most readily recognized intellectual—conservative or Liberal—in America. From the early 1950s, when as *enfant terrible* he assaulted his alma mater, godless, Liberal Yale, with a rude book (*God and Man at Yale*) just before assaulting political Liberalism nationwide with his rude magazine (*National Review*), Bill remained a figure even into the 1990s. Whereupon it seemed he spent the entire decade retiring, giving one last public appearance over and again. He had a lot to retire from: the lecture circuit (seventy or so lectures yearly), his television show (weekly for thirty-three years), and his magazine. Through all these decades, as issues and fashions changed, Bill adapted. He had a prevenient sense for the shifting currents of the Zeitgeist and an uncanny sense of how to latch onto enough bits of it to remain a figure. In so doing he enlarged conservatism's voice across the country and kept it current with the public discourse.

He was a great man. On this most who knew him agreed. I first proffered this judgment in *The Conservative Crack-Up* and prepared to defend my claim against the critics' onslaught, but I received no complaints, possibly because I filed a few caveats about that greatness. Yet, all great men let us down here and there, and as the 1970s gave way to the 1980s, he disappointed me and other movement conservatives prominent in the 1960s generation. He retired from political activism without telling those of us who thought of him as our leader. Not that he ever gave up his brutal schedule. He died bent over the desk in the messy office he kept in the garage of his Stamford home. He was eighty-two. After burning the candle at both ends for a lifetime, Bill had been in dreadful physical decline for years. I had not expected his appalling physical decline. For the first thirty years that I knew him, he was an intellectual marvel in perpetual motion.

We had become friends toward the end of his *enfant terrible* days in the late 1960s, when I was turning my off-campus magazine at Indiana University into the national magazine of the antiradical student movement. He was a frequent participant in our programs both at IU and on other campuses. His arrival was always a whirlwind. One afternoon in 1968, as he thrilled scores of students crammed into our dilapidated offices, whose walls we had painted Paris green in imitation of his *National Review* offices, a local professor turned to me and pointed to Bill. Sitting atop my desk, waving a cigar, the conservative movement's most conspicuous leader was joking, and laughing, enthralling his young admirers with the nonsense of the world. Observed the professor: "He'll look that youthful forever." Laughter was an additive to the conservative movement that the whole Buckley family prescribed. Bill was not the only Buckley fortifying the conservative movement. There were brothers and sisters, at least two of whom were journalists as was his youngest brother, Reid, the family chronicler. His brother Jim would become a United States senator and federal judge. They were all literate, intelligent, and enormously entertaining. Bill's charming sister, Priscilla, the managing editor at *National Review* for twenty-eight years, once counseled me to *"never"* give up on humor.

That afternoon in my office, Bill was forty-three years old, but the professor was to be proved terribly wrong. When Bill died, he had been suffering one ailment after another: skin cancer, diabetes, sleep apnea, heart and prostate problems, and emphysema—he smoked cigars (often Cuban) all his life, and with his characteristic abandon he *inhaled* them! On that 1968 visit he insisted on seeing the varsity pool, where I had trained with the fabled Olympians and world record holders of Doc Counsilman's legendary swim teams (Australian Olympian John Marshall, had been one of Bill's Yale roommates). He wanted to pop into a local bar, the Stardust, where allegedly (and inaccurately) Hoagy Carmichael wrote "Stardust." "The greatest jazz song of the twentieth century," Bill enthused. As we left for my office across the street, I heard the bartender say "Bill Buckley just came in with some flunky." That flunky would be me.

That night in debate, Bill mopped up the stage with a celebrated Liberal prodigy, a professor whose works had appeared in both scholarly journals and *Playboy*. In an era when debate was still a serious event on campus, Bill was probably the most formidable debater in the country—an item lost in all the obituaries I read about him in 2008. The prof he debated that night at Indiana University was a star on the faculty of the department of history and philosophy of science, who advocated sex, drugs, pacifism, personal liberation—the whole 1960s hippie buffet, though he himself was a teetotaler and vegetarian. If I recall correctly, even coffee was off his personal menu, though he adored Pepperidge Farm cookies and kept his cupboard well stocked—one of his undergraduate girlfriends was a friend of mine, and though he was middle-aged, we all partied together—possibly a criminal offense on campuses today, where every bulletin board has "Rape" warnings posted.

The prof was much like Charles Reich, who in his 1970 best seller, *The Greening of America*, served as the pied piper of 1960s youthful carnality, despite being, even in middle age, a virgin. Somehow after the fame of *Greening*, Charlie discovered that his male organ was not meant solely for urination but was, as today's techies might say, a dual-use technology. *Eee-yow*, he became a homosexual and drug user somewhere in California and the author of an even sillier book than *Greening*, namely, *The Sorcerer of Bolinas Reef*. Within years all Charlie's prophetic rumble bumble would be overtaken by the Carter administration's drear and something utterly unforeseen by Charlie even in the delirious pages of *Sorcerer*, the Reagan Revolution. In fact, the hippie apocalypse is today remembered only for its legacy of increased drug addiction, mental illness, venereal disease, and a short spike in petty crime. University life also suffered a decline in serious scholarship and a rise in trivial studies: "The History of Rock and Roll," "Comic Books as Literature," "Feminist Studies," and "African-American Studies." Possibly there are courses on the hula hoop. I am only familiar with the most prominent American universities.

After Bill's debate we piled into the jalopies college students drove in those days and headed for an old farmhouse that my roommates and I lived in out on the hilly Hoosier countryside. There the local members of Young Americans for Freedom (YAF) and the Intercollegiate Studies Institute (ISI) partied with Bill in the bar, a room featuring huge posters from the Goldwater campaign and bar stools made from sawed-off tree trunks. Even after a two-hour debate, Bill was ebullient into the wee hours. Early the next morning, I was awakened by his telephone call from the Indianapolis airport an hour or so away. Already he was on his way to his next lecture, but he had promised an article for us, and here he was, ready to dictate it before his early morning flight. His dictation was flawless. My head was throbbing.

In those days the conservative movement was a tight-knit group. There were rivalries, for instance, between libertarian rigorists and the equally rigorous traditionalists, but most of us shared a camaraderie that bound the movement together as we developed the ideas and policies of American conservatism . . . and the polemics. In the early days many of us followed in Bill's footsteps, polemicizing against Liberalism and its ugly cousin, the radical left, known in the 1960s as the New Left. Bill and the colleagues he brought together at *National Review*, such as Frank Meyer and Russell Kirk, composed the first generation of conservatism. We members of YAF and ISI composed the next generation. The members of the older generation were our mentors.

When Meyer died in 1972, Bill's secretary, Frances Bronson, called my office in Indiana and arranged for me to ride with Bill and several others in his limousine (he relished an entourage) to the service at Frank's home in rural upstate New York. Along the way Bill did dictation and stopped at a rest area to telephone in his syndicated column, which he had composed in the car on a portable typewriter, famously in about twenty minutes. The laptop and Internet were then unimaginable even to Bill, who relished every leap in technology, though the leaps in those days were few compared with the stupendous leaps of the 1990s and early twenty-first century.

Bill rarely slowed down back then, when he served as the conservative movement's herald. He was joyous, highly intellectual, and still a self-confessed radical *individualist*—early in the movement the term *individualist* was preferred by conservatives, particularly those of a libertarian stripe. With the Nixon administration, however, he was entering the next phase of his career, his political phase during which he served as a player in national Republican politics. Still, during Nixon's first term Bill remained, at least in the eyes of young conservatives, a movement activist.

The tight-knit nature of the movement would be lost

as the years stretched on and conservatism became more of a mass movement. The camaraderie of the generations evanesced. As the generation following mine began its climb, careerism and opportunism seized enough of the newcomers to validate Eric Hoffer's diagnosis of the degeneration of a great cause into "a business," then into "a racket." It took years for me to notice the degeneration, though with the conviction of frauds such as Jack Abramoff, Rep. Randall "Duke" Cunningham, and Rep. Bob Ney during the presidency of George W. Bush, and the embarrassments suffered by some of the personalities—William Bennett, author of *The Book of Virtues*, running up $8 million gambling tabs in Las Vegas,[4] for example—the degeneration should have been apparent.

Al Regnery, my contemporary and since the late 1950s a movement activist, has reminded me of the friendly solidarity we all shared. He recalls YAF's tenth anniversary held in 1970 at the Buckley family estate in Sharon, Connecticut, where YAF's founding document, the Sharon Statement, had been drawn up. Hundreds of us returned to mingle with Bill and his *National Review* colleagues. "We all knew each other and got along," Al recollected in an interview for this book. There was very little rivalry, certainly no generational rivalry, and by 1970 we were even bringing along conservatism's third generation.

To Sharon I brought the teenaged Bill Kristol. Kristol's contemporary, Christopher Buckley, was there too. Christopher is Bill's only child. Both young men were destined for great things by middle age. Of the two, Kristol was more outspokenly conservative, and though younger than the rest of us, he participated actively in the lectures and bull sessions. Christopher was hesitant. In fact, he was painfully uncomfortable and blinking nervously, that being a congenital tic of his that over the years comes and goes. Even then this unhappy prodigy had more hang-ups than a telemarketer. Al has reminded me of another facet of the conservative mind-set in those days: we had no hint of the huge political success that we would achieve a decade later when our leader, ex-governor Ronald Reagan, would vanquish President Carter and what was left of cracked-up Liberalism. "We thought we might pick up a congressional seat here or there," Al recalls, but "we thought we would not be much more than a thorn in the Liberal Establishment's side, probably forever."[5]

By the early twenty-first century, Al had left Regnery Publishing, having rung up a record of best sellers unsurpassed by any publisher of equivalent size in American publishing history, and had become publisher of the *American Spectator*. By then our movement had achieved far more than we had thought possible back in 1970. President Reagan had become one of the greatest presidents of the twentieth century, and on a drizzly June day in 2004, we found ourselves standing side by side at his stately service at the National Cathedral. Down the aisle walked Lady Thatcher and scores of conservative dignitaries whose statures we could not have imagined at the Buckley estate on the tenth anniversary of YAF, despite all our combative spirits. Now, four years later, here we were in St. Patrick's for Bill's funereal honors. Together we were about to witness a poignant reminder of the degeneration that, over the course of the Bush administration, weakened our movement.

There were only two eulogists, Henry Kissinger, from Bill's generation, and Christopher, from the movement's third generation. The differences in their presentations exposed starkly the corrosion that easy celebrity had imposed on the movement's standards. First up was former secretary of state Henry Kissinger, Bill's great friend (and I am proud to say mine too; when the Clinton government was after me in the late 1990s, with grand jury inquiries and lapdog journalists menacing the First Amendment, Henry was a loyal defender). Henry is not a movement conservative but surely a proven conservative in the historic sense. Where Henry was dignified and wise, Christopher was flippant. Henry moved us to deep emotion, Christopher to laughter. In fewer than a thousand eloquent words, Henry superbly captured Bill's life.[6] Christopher hardly said anything worth quoting.

Before choking up, the eighty-five-year-old statesman said in his deep basso profundo:

> Bill Buckley inspired a political movement that changed American politics; he founded the *National Review* that, for over a generation, has shaped American political discussion; he hosted an influential talk show for thirty [thirty-three] years; he wrote an elegant column . . .

A man of such stunning versatility might have proved daunting to those around him. Yet we mourn him for his civility even to adversaries, his conviviality, his commitment and, above all, the way he infused our lives with a very special presence . . .

With what zest Bill lived his life. There was never quite enough time to fulfill all the possibilities that his many gifts opened to him. He was endlessly peripatetic: Winters in Gstaad; summers in Connecticut; sailing trips to the Caribbean or across the Atlantic and Pacific Oceans; even the compulsion to leave every dinner party by ten o'clock. He worked ebulliently at the causes towards which his moral convictions impelled him, and he did so with a sense of wonder—and perhaps a little awe—that a kind of miracle had vouchsafed him the opportunity to enjoy so much what was driven by inner necessity . . .

In the solitude of parting, all of us give thanks to a benign Providence that enabled us to walk part of our way with this noble, gentle and valiant man who was very truly touched by the grace of God.[7]

A stupendous summing-up, and that last line does trigger the fugitive thought: did Bill ever grow out of surreptitiously baptizing his friends?

Then came Christopher. It later was revealed that he had spent the last year or so attending to two dying parents, his imperious and beautiful socialite mother, Pat, who died on April 15, 2007, and his father, who was devastated by the death of his wife of fifty-six years and in dreadful decline, an unbroken descent from the grandeur of his early celebrity to his final horrible decrepitude. Christopher, from a fusion of deep love and darker emotions, had attended to them dutifully and, one concludes from his memoir that was soon to appear, almost solitarily.

Over lunch a few years before, he had told me of his parents' unhappy, indeed angry, deterioration, pledging me to silence. I kept my word, and now it appears that I could have written a best seller if I put down all that I found out about this great conservative leader's final act. Of course, that would be but another instance of a conservative getting ahead by sniping at another conservative. I resisted the impulse. Christopher did not.

For several years I said not a word, though Bill's infirmities were apparent whenever I saw him. As for Christopher, from his eulogy at St. Patrick's onward to the publication of his astonishing book a year later, *Losing Mum and Pup: A Memoir*, he blurted it all out in lurid detail. What is more, in the months between his eulogy and publication of his 2009 book, Christopher would manifest all the pernicious qualities that the opportunists, most notably the Reformed Conservatives (RCs), were to manifest in exploiting the conservative movement's postelection time of troubles. In the period between his eulogy and the appearance of his book, Christopher: (1) endorsed the most left-wing and ill-prepared Democratic presidential candidate ever, while insisting that Barack Obama would be, if elected, too intelligent to attempt "traditional left-politics"[8]; (2) joined in the Palin hysteria; (3) provoked a break with *National Review*; and (4) ridiculed Rush Limbaugh after Rush broadcast a eulogy to Bill, Christopher's most cruel line being "Rush, you're no William F. Buckley, Jr."[9]

Christopher had always been coy about just what sort of conservative he might be. In 2008 he revealed himself to be an RC of the fellow-traveler variety. What is more, he became another political know-it-all, displaying the usual self-absorption, opportunism, lust for attention, intellectual sloppiness, and treachery of the RCs. Beyond that, he displayed the spoiled child's desire to have it both ways. He would be Bill's loving son and a louse. "Being a devious little s—" is how he introduced one of the perfidious family revelations in his book.[10]

The sorry act began on the altar at St. Patrick's. There Christopher's transgression was mostly ill-advised flippancy. In the intimacy of the family, he often called his father "Pup." He might have also called him "S—head," but neither S—head nor Pup was quite right for this occasion. The continual repetition of this condescending nickname made many wince. Christopher went on to tell a few amusing jokes, including this rather grisly anecdote: "When we held the wake for him some days after he died, I placed inside his casket a few items to see him across the River Styx: a favorite rosary, the TV remote control—private joke—a jar of peanut butter, and my mother's ashes. I can hear her saying, 'Bill—what is that disgusting substance leaking all over me.'"[11] As I say, next to Henry's eloquence, Christopher did not leave much worth quoting, save for this: "He [Bill] was—inarguably— a great man. This is, from a son's perspective, a mixed blessing, because it means having to share him with the wide world."[12]

So here is part of the explanation for Christopher's disloyalty. He felt himself to be the neglected son, who, as the eulogy suggested and the book made clear, envied his father's superior talents. Okay, I sympathize, but by the age of fifty-five, anyone but a Me Generation narcissist should be able to get over such a grudge or at least be gentleman enough to squelch the impulse to exploit his father's condition. What is it that we are told about not speaking ill of the dead, who are no longer around to defend themselves?

Instead this self-proclaimed "devious little s—" blabbed on in his memoir about his father's loss of memory, his failure to differentiate the DVD from the thermostat, his plans for luncheons with friends long deceased, and the old man's proclivity for urinating in public. Hell, Christopher, back at the farmhouse in 1968, after a few beers in the cool of the night, your father urinated off of our front porch. His motto might have been "Void Where Prohibited." Perhaps the most appalling of the aggrieved son's revelations is that he leaned over his comatose mother's deathbed and said, "I forgive you."[13] What if she was not fully comatose, Christopher? Would you want that to be her last memory of you as she shoved off across your River Styx? If you really have forgiven her, why did you write this book?*

In an era of cheap celebrity, Christopher calibrated quite astutely that such revelations will ensure a few more moments of fame. Britney Spears and Paris Hilton probably make similar calculations. If you look across the national landscape today, you will not see many replications of what Aristotle envisaged as the great-souled man.

At St. Patrick's, after betraying some of the deep anger he bore his father, along with the manifest deep love, the conflicted Christopher went on to quote by way of epitaph a few moving lines from Robert Louis Stevenson's "Requiem." He might have better chosen Longfellow's lines from "The Ladder of St. Augustine." They are more apposite:

> The heights by great men reached and kept
>   Were not attained by sudden flight,
> But they, while their companions slept,
>   *Were toiling upward in the night.*

As perhaps the founder most critical to the growth of the modern conservative movement, Bill toiled like no one

---

*Christopher is not a particularly reliable reporter. Recalling a mix-up between his father and President-elect Reagan in late 1980, Christopher told his father's biographer, John Judis, that Reagan "had begun at this point to lose it a little, so he could be excused for not remembering things." Fortunately for the country, the mentally impaired president had an easy eight years ahead of him. This extravagance can be found on page 424 of Judis's *William F. Buckley, Jr.: Patron Saint of the Conservatives.*

I have ever known. Henry captured a sense of it in his eulogy, but there was more. From the 1950s through the 1980s, Bill's achievements are milestones in the growth of American conservatism. Retailing them here will record the movement's trek from the political fringe in the 1950s to political center stage, while giving Bill the credit owed him.

After the publication of *God and Man at Yale* in 1951, Bill gathered a diverse group of anti-Communists, libertarians, and traditionalists to found *National Review* in 1955. The magazine's publisher through much of its early life, William Rusher, has recorded that "Buckley brought us all together—Russell Kirk, Frank Meyer, and all sorts of libertarians and traditionalists, and anti-Communists just like myself and [Whittaker] Chambers, who all had in common that the liberals were their great enemies but, very often, did not have much else in common and, indeed, regarded each other as rivals."[14] Two years before, in 1953, Bill helped found the intellectual wing of conservatism's youth movement, ISI, becoming its first president. In 1960 he helped found YAF, the conservative youth movement's organization for political activists. YAF was soon opposing the New Left's rough equivalent of it, Students for a Democratic Society (SDS) on campus and occasionally in street demonstrations.

In 1964, within days of the Goldwater defeat, Bill joined with a small group of conservatives to found the American Conservative Union (ACU), the conservatives' answer to the Liberals' national political organization, Americans for Democratic Action (ADA). In 1965, when the conservative movement was ready to challenge Liberal domination of New York City, Bill was tapped to run for mayor on the newly founded New York Conservative Party ticket, another conservative group he helped to found. He won only 13 percent of the vote, but with élan and high intelligence, he attracted national attention to conservatism's political viability. Regnery, in his history of American conservatism, adjudges Bill's mayoral campaign one of the three most important political campaigns in the history of modern conservatism, along with the presidential campaigns of Goldwater in 1964 and of Governor Ronald Reagan in 1980.[15]

For Bill personally the mayoral race made him a permanent national figure until his retirement, whenever that was actually finalized. His nationally syndicated column, soon to be one of the country's most popular, began in 1962. Four years later he started *Firing Line*, which at the time of its discontinuance was the country's longest-playing television talk show. Over the decades Bill would write more than fifty books, some six thousand columns, and innumerable articles and book reviews. Beyond the writing was the theater: some fifteen hundred broadcasts of *Firing Line*, along with the years of lectures and debates. He also appeared on all the popular late-night television talk shows, something that no serious intellectual is invited to do nowadays. At Yale, where his papers are archived, they cover 550 linear feet of filing cabinets.

Just as Bill's career achievements mark milestones in conservatism's development, the phases that he went through highlight the intellectual and political evolution of the country from conservatism's birth in the 1950s to the disappointments of the late Bush years in the early twenty-first century. His career had four phases. First was his period as the *enfant terrible*, which we have discussed. Next was his more conventional political phase, during which he was surprisingly close to President Richard Nixon, despite Nixon's intentional distancing of himself from the conservative movement. Bill advised Nixon to take John Gardner, a paradigmatic Liberal, as his 1968 running mate and eventually suggested two other Liberal Republicans for Nixon's cabinet, Governors Nelson Rockefeller and William Scranton. He encouraged such solid movement conservatives as Frank Shakespeare to campaign for Nixon and join his administration. Shakespeare eventually became the head of Nixon's United States Information Agency. As for Bill, he accepted minor posts in the administration and became America's public delegate to the United Nations, a position Eleanor Roosevelt once held.

Yet, Bill's sense of the shifting Zeitgeist was uncanny. The spirit of the age was dropping old values and picking up new ones. The value placed on intellect weakened in the 1970s, eventually to be replaced by nothing more elevated than the art of being seen in public memorably, perhaps wearing tennis shoes while at a black-tie function or possibly giving the finger to the pope. Essential to the art was the presence of a camera crew or at least a photographer. The spread of mass communications played a role in this degeneracy, as did, of course, vulgar egalitarianism. Bill somehow sensed the change. The intellectual, while rarely being a commanding figure in America, was slipping further in prominence, now being vastly overshadowed by the inane celebrity.

Bill's plan to write a major intellectual work modeled on José Ortega y Gasset's *The Revolt of the Masses*, which he had put on hold in the mid-1960s, was now out of the question. He began the decade talking about mounting a Conservative Party campaign for Robert Kennedy's old Senate seat and using it as a springboard to a presidential campaign. But by the mid-1970s that was as unthinkable as the major intellectual book. His biographer, John Judis, writes that Bill resolved, about this time, to write a novel, sail his sailboat across the Atlantic, and perform Bach on his harpsichord with a professional orchestra.[16] Eventually he did all this, and when he crossed the Atlantic a second time under sail, he brought along a professional photographer for a *People* magazine spread—this just before the Republican Party nominated Ronald Reagan. In 1985 he duplicated the feat in the Pacific. He also wrote novels, launched a new brand of peanut butter (P.B., "the first peanut butter for grown-ups"), buzzed the *Titanic* in a diving bell, performed Bach with the Phoenix Symphony, and painted. He painted pretty well for an amateur. I cherish a painting that he pulled from his wall late one night after cigars and port in his living room on Seventy-third Street. Appropriately it is a painting of a lone sailboat gleaming in the moonlight.

Aside from the shifting Zeitgeist, what ended Bill's political phase and began his Phase III was Watergate. Bill had always been a fiercely loyal friend, and so he was to Nixon. He stuck by him during the Watergate revelations, believing in Nixon's innocence and in the unfairness of the Democrats' attacks until the autumn of 1973. Bill was stunned by the brutality he saw at the end of the Watergate scandal and by the devious partisanship of both sides. Richard Brookhiser, one of Bill's former protégés, recalls an evening prior to the 1984 election when, during an editorial dinner at the Buckleys' Seventy-third Street pied-à-terre, there was serious discussion of Bill running for president if President Reagan did not seek reelection.[17]

Perhaps his guests were serious, but I doubt Bill was. By 1984 Bill was well into his Phase III, and politics took second place to the rigors of the Zeitgeist: sailing the ocean waves, writing novels, launching a new peanut butter. Bill was no longer a political player but a personality, one adulated by conservatives; but no longer was he serious about advancing the conservative movement. He was in and out of his friend Ronald Reagan's White House, but more as a celebrity than the kind of political player he was in the Nixon White House.

I shall expand on this shortly, but first consider how different the Nixon White House was from the Reagan White House. It was a difference spawned not only by the different characters of the presidents but by the different interests of their eras. The Nixon White House maintained a distance from the conservative movement, while the Reagan White House was home to a movement conservative, the longtime

National Review reader, President Reagan. Nonetheless, the Nixon White House was at least selectively open to conservative ideas, while the Reagan White House was divided by warring factions, the movement conservatives led by Ed Meese and Martin Anderson, and the country club Republicans led by Mike Deaver and James Baker. We now know that President Reagan was assiduous in implementing a historic, if narrow, agenda; but the factionalism of his government distracted it from other matters, one being the creation of a conservative counterculture. Incidentally, by the presidency of George W. Bush, no such factionalism existed in the White House. The ongoing growth of conservatism had overwhelmed the country club Republicans, though now there were new threats to conservatism, namely, corruption and a debilitating smugness.

Contrary to what one might think from reading the popular appraisals of the Nixon administration, the presidency was very open to intellectuals, which probably reflects the higher intellectuality of the 1960s as compared with the decades to come—witness Dr. Henry Kissinger heading the National Security Council and Dr. Daniel Patrick Moynihan as Nixon's counselor for urban affairs.

At the time Pat Moynihan was one of those apostate Liberals who had been, as his friend Irving Kristol put it, "mugged by reality." Thus Pat was a neoconservative, critical of the Great Society's excesses and absorbed with the consequences, for instance, the "urban crisis" involving urban crime, poverty, dependence on government programs, and other underclass pathologies. These were perceived as

the major domestic problems of the time, and the neoconservatives analyzed them in their publications
(*Commentary* and a quarterly that Irving founded, *The
Public Interest*). The neoconservatives also brought their
analysis of the era's domestic problems into mainstream
media where they, being mostly New York and Cambridge
intellectuals, still were welcome.

As editor of the *American Spectator*, I was one of the
first movement conservatives to welcome them to conservatism. Bill welcomed them too. Some movement conservatives were suspicious of these wandering Liberals, but Bill
and I were friendly with Irving, Pat, and the others. Pat,
alas, returned to Liberalism after being elected to the Senate
in 1976, beating Bill's brother, Senator Jim Buckley. Nonetheless, in the Nixon years and for a while thereafter, he was
a friend and even a mentor. To this day I have occasion to
quote his wise reservations about bureaucracy's excesses or
the limits of social policy. Signed copies of his books remain
in my library, and in my son's home is an engraved silver
cup that Pat sent him from India while serving as American
ambassador when my Patrick was born. When Pat died in
2003, his neoconservative past was mostly ignored in the
obituaries, this being the way Liberals create a mythical history of their country, a history devoid of thoughtful conservatives. It is one of the reasons they are flabbergasted
when conservatives best them in debate or on election day.

The movement conservatives' suspicions of the neoconservatives were based in part on the neoconservatives'
being more comfortable with the welfare state than were

limited-government conservatives. To be sure, the neo-conservatives remained vigilant of government's excesses and "unintended consequences," but at least some still hoped to channel the welfare state toward conservative values, an aspiration not far removed from the hopes of Russell Kirk's 1950s traditionalists.

The neoconservatives also took a strong stand against the Soviet Union and opponents of democracy at the United Nations. As our UN ambassador, Pat, and later Jeane Kirkpatrick, were stirring in their defense of what Pat called "the party of liberty." Toward the end of the Carter administration's foreign policy disasters, Jeane wrote a piece in *Commentary* outlining the kind of foreign policy that would contain our international enemies, "Dictatorships and Double Standards."[18] It attracted the eye of candidate Reagan and earned her a place in his government. By Reagan's election the neoconservatives were firmly in the conservative camp. Pat was then exiting stage left, but he was being replaced by such apostate Liberals as Harvard's Professor James Q. Wilson and the Podhoretzes, Norman and his wife, Midge Decter. Midge was to join the board of the Heritage Foundation. Kirkpatrick, after leaving the UN, joined the board of the *American Spectator*.

Throughout the 1970s the neoconservatives' influence grew within the conservative movement, even as it waned in mainstream media. When Reagan entered 1600 Pennsylvania Avenue in 1981, the neoconservatives were part of the conservative team challenging the Republican Party's country clubbers, but with different consequences than during the Nixon years. There was no Pat Moynihan at Reagan's side, and Irving, who had once been rumored to be Pat's replacement as domestic adviser in the Nixon administration,[19] was only known to have set foot in the White House when he came as my guest to a luncheon the president asked me to arrange with conservative intellectuals. Irving *was* influential in choosing some of the administration's appointees, most famously William Bennett at the National Endowment for the Humanities over the traditionalist conservatives' choice, Professor Mel Bradford of the University of Dallas. Yet Irving, one of the most influential conservatives the late twentieth century, was not the celebrated figure he and his neoconservative newcomers to conservatism were in the Nixon years.

The reason, I suspect, was the drift of the Zeitgeist. In the Reagan years, intellect and intellectuals such as Irving were out. Socialites and the charity-ball conservatives were in. Irving Kristol was a less prominent guest at the White House than Betsy Bloomingdale, a kind of Bernard Baruch of the Reagan years. Betsy was the rich socialite wife of Alfred Bloomingdale, a member of Reagan's California kitchen cabinet. She was expert in designer dresses, interior décor, and charity balls. She was championed by Nancy Reagan, who shared many of her interests and was, of course, a force in the Reagan White House, where she sided not with Meese and Anderson but with Deaver and Baker. Nancy was also a friend of Pat Buckley, a charity-ball conservative of formidable accomplishments. None of the charity-ball conservatives had much interest in the urban crisis, save when their limousines were in the shop and they had to hail a taxi.

They were, however, a force in the 1980s, perhaps being the pretense for Liberals to designate it a decade of "glitz," another example of Liberals creating a mythic history. The 1980s were no glitzier than the Clintons' 1990s. In fact, the Reagans' Hollywoodians were fewer, and their moneyed visitors were more likely socialites and entrepreneurs than the rastaquouères making illegal campaign contributions in the Clinton White House. Bill was quick to pick up on the influence of the charity-ball conservatives. His wife, Pat, had long been one of Manhattan's most frequently quoted socialites, widely read in the gossip columns of "Suzy" and Liz Smith. If there had been a Bartlett's *Familiar Quotations by Socialites*, Pat would have appeared even more frequently than Betsy. By the 1980s Bill's name popped up in the gossip columns with increasing frequency, certainly more frequently than back during his Phase I or Phase II periods. Once again Bill's prevenient sense of the Zeitgeist kept him current.

Of course, politically speaking, the charity-ball conservatives played little role in the policies of the Reagan years. Their role was cultural. Meanwhile, and sometimes almost alone, the Old Cowboy advanced his limited, if historic agenda: the defeat of Communism, the revival of the economy through tax cuts, and the reduction of government regulation. It is worth remembering that notwithstanding the achievements of the conservatives and the neoconservatives, a good many of them were profoundly critical of

Reagan during his presidency. Bill was particularly critical of Reagan's late 1980s diplomatic initiatives with the Soviet Union. Irving was too. Yet the Old Cowboy knew what he was about. As a legacy, he left a generation of unsurpassed economic growth in a world free of great power hostilities.

The achievements of the Reagan administration were the consequence of thirty years of the conservative movement's development—that and something else. Let us not forget the crack-up of Liberalism, or as the historian Sean Wilentz diagnosed it, the fragmentation. It entailed radicalization and the domination of practically every Liberal constituency by its most fevered cadres. As a consequence of Liberalism's fragmentation and radicalization, the era of the late 1970s was suddenly propitious for the arrival of a New Order similar to the New Order that Liberals had recognized a generation earlier with FDR's election and banishment of the Republicans' Old Order. Worth recalling is that not all conservatives thought the septuagenarian Reagan was up to ushering in a New Order in 1980. They regretted that he had not been elected in 1976 when he might have been more vigorous. Bill was among them. In the late 1970s he was actually sympathetic to the presidential ambitions of a distinctly nonmovement conservative, George H. W. Bush.[20] Irving was even more dubious of a 1980 Reagan candidacy. I recall his refusing to attend a dinner I gave at Manhattan's Union League Club in 1978 to introduce Governor Reagan to the neoconservatives. His fellow neoconservatives, the Podhoretzes of *Commentary* and Nathan Glazer of the *Public Interest*, did attend it and left impressed.

Yet, if Reagan might have been more vigorous in 1976, so, too, would Liberalism have been more vigorous in resisting him. Reagan's successful commencement of a New Order validates an insight from nineteenth-century Swiss historian Jacob Burckhardt, filed away in his essay "On Fortune and Misfortune." There he writes that "from time to time a great event, ardently desired, does not take place because some future time will fulfill it in greater perfection."[21]

Reagan's election in 1980 fulfilled "in greater perfection" an event we conservatives ardently desired, namely, a conservative political ascendancy, but though a boon to the economy and to world peace, our political ascendancy had almost no influence on the political culture of the country. The *Kultursmog*, cited at the outset of this book, remained dominated by the Liberals, and as it was the preserve of an increasingly radicalized Liberalism, their growing radicalization made the *smog* ever more resistant to reason or even to disagreement. Supply-side economics was rendered derisory in the *smog*. Reagan was rendered a bungling, lazy simpleton on the brink of nuclear war. The conservatives whose politics had been vindicated by Reagan's successes were culturally marginalized and actually branded "extremists," despite what would prove to be years of successful governance.

The fact is that during Reagan's presidency his White House did almost nothing to influence the *Kultursmog*, a challenge that set back Reagan's New Order and impeded the conservative movement's ability to grow for the next two decades. Here is but another example of conservatism's limited political libido. At the end of the president's first term, Herb London, at the time a dean on the faculty of New York University, recalls being tasked as a member of the Committee for the Next Agenda to write up a report suggesting what might be done upon the president's reelection. Working with such conservative stalwarts as Martin Anderson, Ed Feulner, and Ed Meese, he tendered a report featuring recommendations for domestic policy and foreign policy. But he and his fellow members were also mindful of the *Kultursmog*'s influence on politics and the public discourse. They were intent on, as we might say, clearing the air by establishing a conservative counterculture. London personally urged Reagan and his supporters to set up institutions to influence the political culture. The president seemed interested, London recalls. He read the report, studiously underlining significant sections.

Aside, however, from Reagan's underlining, London got no support either inside the government or from Reagan's kitchen cabinet. London suggested the establishment of media outlets. He envisaged the funding of publications and their cooperation with conservative think tanks, all exchanging ideas, interests, and enthusiasms. London had no takers. When he approached conservative businesspeople (Alfred Bloomingdale was among them!), they assured him that all they had to do to maintain the conservative ascendancy was to fund political campaigns. The cultural forces that shaped the issues and the rhetoric of politics need not be confronted with a conservative challenge.[22] It is, however, axiomatic that there can be no lasting political change without cultural change—the former rests on the latter and will teeter without a solid foundation.

A little later, I attempted the same mission with Bill, unaware that now he was purely a personality, his only political activity being his syndicated column and the editorship of *National Review*. In the autumn of 1986, he had me to a dinner with his editors, once again at his elegant Seventy-third Street pied-à-terre. I told him that there was a perceptible drifting apart among the once tight-knit movement conservatives, the writers, the scholars, the editors. We were not taking an interest in each other's work, reviewing each other's books, analyzing each other's ideas. It appeared to me that it was now, as I said, "every man for himself." We had the magazines, the writers, the think tanks, for what in those days I actually called a "conservative counterculture," whose job it would be to purify the *Kultursmog*.

"What would you have us do?" Bill blandly inquired, the air of his dining room hazy with cigar smoke, the ambiance mellowed by brandy. I responded, "Take an interest in each other's work." The great entertainer of the 1980s, with timing reminiscent of a climactic moment on *Firing Line*, replied, "*That* would be boring." I was no more successful with *National Review*'s editor in chief than London was with the businessmen. Bill would never want to hurt a friend. Shortly after my futile evening, he wrote me a kind letter, concluding that it had been many years since he was "much inclined as an activist."[23] At any rate there were charity balls to attend, and soon he undertook a flight around the world on the supersonic Concorde, with ninety-five fans paying $39,800 a seat.[24]

In the late 1980s, the continued growth of the conservative movement was grinding to a halt. Soon it would be challenged by a Democratic takeover of the White House. The conservative political ascendancy would remain fragile until its political victories could be matched by victories in the political culture. It was time to create the institutions essential for a conservative counterculture. By 2008 the institutions would be in place, as we shall see.

SMEARED BY THE SMOG

The Zeitgeist, the *Kultursmog*, and the Sidelining of Conservatism

F ame," Milton tells us, is "that last infirmity of noble mind."[1] Well, William F. Buckley Jr. earned his fame legitimately. He earned it by adhering to the first principle of the conservative movement, individual liberty. He lived individual liberty and advocated it for others. Through all the phases of his life, even his nonpolitical ones, he was a nineteenth-century individualist wedded to reason, empiricism, and the virtues as he perceived them. Yet by the early 1990s Bill reviewed the Zeitgeist, as was his custom, and my guess is he found it so void of intellect that he said to himself, "Oh, the hell with it." He had buzzed the *Titanic*. He had suffered through the P.B. peanut butter launch. For this Renaissance man, that was about as far into celebrity self-promotion as he would go. The shifts in the Zeitgeist had consequences for the conservative movement too.

The Zeitgeist, as conceived of in the eighteenth century by the German philosophers Herder and Hegel, is usually translated the "spirit of the age." In it are packed all sorts of phenomena: ideas, sentiments, morals, fashions, the idiot impulse that impelled that teenager back in 1992 to ask Bill Clinton on MTV about his underpants, and the impulse that impelled him to answer—whether truthfully or not, only Monica Lewinsky and a few thousand slutty females really know. As with all spirits, the spirit of the age is intangible, and so are its ever-changing contents: ideas, sentiments, morals, fashions, and so forth. That the spirit of the age exists and that it is changeable over time is obvious because we can see its consequences: changing fashions, changing values, changing undergarments. Would any previous president have discussed his underpants in public? Would any member of an earlier audience pose the Underpants Query? Obviously the Zeitgeist's values and desiderata had changed tremendously by the 1990s, and the change was not edifying.

The problem with the Zeitgeist for Bill Buckley during Phase IV was that it had almost no appreciation for intellect, which perhaps explains some of the problems that conservatism, too, faced during the presidency of George W. Bush. As we have seen, the conservative movement was founded on intellect and absorbed with the play of ideas: libertarian ideas, ideas about tradition, the Constitution, free markets. Throughout the 1970s and 1980s, these ideas gained purchase on the Republican Party, provoking Senator Daniel Patrick Moynihan to observe in 1980, "All of a sudden the GOP has become a party of ideas"[2]

Unfortunately, by the 1990s intellect was as passé as the powdered wig. To be sure, intellect was alive and energetic in some areas of American life, for instance, among the wizards of Silicon Valley, but in politics and culture intellect was on sabbatical. Worse still for conservatism, though the administration of George W. Bush was basically conservative, conservatism's fundamental ideas were being ignored, most importantly individual liberty and limited government. Admittedly, the Bush administration was strong on traditional values, forceful foreign policy (though after the Iraq invasion the conservative consensus fragmented on what this meant), and conservative judicial appointments. Yet the administration was insouciant about what matters most to movement conservatives, personal liberty and limited government.

In fact, during the Bush administration these fundamental ideas were dismissed as somehow dated. David Brooks propounded something he called "National Greatness Conservatism," and President Bush's chief speechwriter, Michael Gerson, called for "Heroic Conservatism," which sounds like something Richard Wagner might have dreamed up with a very large orchestra behind him, its timpani rumbling madly. After leaving the White House, Gerson used the term as the title for a book that called on conservatives, if they wanted ever again to win elections, to undertake a new New Deal, using the same collectivist means of governance that New Dealers used. About the only thing conservative about Gerson's book was its admiration of things past. Claiming to be an admirer of FDR and Woodrow Wilson, Gerson chided what he called "traditional conservatives" in unctuous terms not unlike those employed by Brooks and the other Reformed Conservatives. His book was not received well by members of the conservative movement, perplexed by why a latter-day New Dealer bothered to call himself a conservative at all. Presumably, Gerson did so for the very same perfectly sensible reason that the RCs called themselves conservatives while kicking conservatives in the shins. Doing so has been a clever marketing technique for years. As I mentioned earlier, soi-disant conservatives can always attract headlines by abusing conservatives.

It all goes back to the conservatives' failure in the 1980s to create a real counterculture of their own. As their ideas spread through government and countrywide, they thought they were winning what Irving Kristol was wont to call the "battle of ideas." In fact, by the 1980s our policy wonks at the various think tanks were more emphatic. In slightly world-weary tones they would say, "We've won the battle of ideas." They had a point. The "stagflation" of the 1970s had been whipped by supply-side tax cuts, deregulation, privatization, monetarism, and a spreading rejection of Keynesian macroeconomics. Conservative solutions for the urban crisis were revitalizing the cities. Soon even the Soviet threat would melt away. Unfortunately the zest for ideas that characterized the neoconservatives and movement conservatives such as Bill Buckley and Milton Friedman was not borne by many Liberals, most of whom insulated themselves from disagreement on the right. In the battle of ideas, Liberals were confirmed noncombatants.

As mentioned in the last chapter, Liberalism has been subjugated by angry cadres. During the 1980s they infiltrated the top spots of the Democratic Party and the country's cultural redoubts. Their dominance of the Democratic Party has assisted in the party's steady decline from 1980 until the midterm elections of 2006, with only Bill Clinton flying the colors of the New Democrats as an intermission. Even then the break lasted but two years before conservatives scored the largest congressional gains in over four decades and forced the New Democrat to admit, "The era of big government is over."[3] As for Liberalism, it remained in the minority even after Barack Obama led the Democratic Party to victory. Five months into Obama's presidency, a Gallup poll found that roughly twice as many Americans were claiming to be conservatives as were claiming to be Liberals.[4] By autumn 2009, conservatives were even more numerous than moderates.[5] On the other hand, wherever the angry Liberals have been able to take power unhindered by the democratic rigmarole, they have usually silenced disagreement and polluted the atmosphere with their indignation. The consequence is the only environmental hazard about which Liberals remain nonchalant. Many consider its pollutants a national treasure. I have in mind the oft-mentioned hazard of *Kultursmog*, which contaminates such vast areas of American culture with Liberal prejudices and bugaboos.

The media, the universities, the arts, government bureaucracy—all these nondemocratic locales are the smokestack industries of *Kultursmog*, and since the Reagan administration, the *smog* has grown ever more poisonous to the free flow of ideas. For some three decades the country's sophisticated culture has been a politicized culture, polluted with the politics of angry Liberalism. Some call it political correctness, but it is more than that. It is a *smog*, hazardous to intellect. The existence of the *Kultursmog* explains two things about contemporary American politics: (1) Liberalism's unchallenged radicalism and (2) the marginalization of conservatives from American culture, particularly conservative intellectuals who might be expected to participate in it.

Ironically, for a political point of view that boasts of its "diversity" Liberalism is a domain reserved for the like-minded. Not surprisingly it gets more like-minded all the time, a process explicated by Cass Sunstein in his book *Going to Extremes: How Like Minds Unite and Divide*. Sunstein, a Liberal himself and a faculty member of the Harvard Law School, has found that congregations of like-minded individuals grow more extreme the more time they spend exclusively in each other's company. Sunstein writes, "When groups go to extremes, it is usually because like-minded people have been able to congregate, often moving from an initial sense of concern to outrage."[6] For years we have seen the outrage at universities, in the arts, even in the supposedly cool and objective realms of media. It was particularly observable during the presidency of George W. Bush when the *Kultursmog* conferred on "the Angry Liberal" a hallowed public status similar to "muckraker" or "humanitarian." In the media reporters seemed to be more outraged by CIA interrogations of enemy combatants than by the atrocities revealed in the interrogations. As Sunstein could have predicted, those pumping their pollutants into the *Kultursmog* have put the *smog* even more out of touch from ordinary American experience, thus explaining why Liberals perceive ordinary Americans as primitive, bigoted, overweight, and incapable of earning a PhD. It is all a matter of the perspective from which one is judging. To a Left-wing *indignado*, the ordinary American is a fascist and pretty stupid.

James Piereson, the former executive director of a foundation famous for sustaining the growth of American conservatism, the John M. Olin Foundation, describes *Kultursmog* as "the Liberal understanding of events ratified as a matter of morals and etiquette" within the media and academe. At another point he summed up *Kultursmog* as "Liberal prejudices built into the culture as truths."[7] The *Kultursmog* is created in two ways: (1) the endless repetition of falsehood and (2) either the complete neglect or the utter misrepresentation of those who do not share Liberalism's values.

Sometimes the repeated falsehoods are small matters of only temporary interest. For instance, during the Liberals' 2009 campaign for healthcare reform, the *Kultursmog* echoed with the claim that 46 million Americans lacked health insurance, despite data from critics showing that the figure was closer to the low 20 millions and possibly much lower. To arrive at the higher figure, Liberals had to throw in 14 million Americans who were eligible for such government programs as Medicaid but simply failed to sign up, another 10 million with incomes above $75,000 who did not want insurance, and those illegal aliens whose status is always in doubt.[8] In the *Kultursmog* the conflicting data were simply ignored.

Other falsehoods are of large enough moment to be repeated through the decades, ultimately to the disfigurement of America's achievement in the world. One particularly egregious repeated falsehood is the claim that America in the late 1940s became hysterical about Communist spies who were for the most part just innocent, peace-loving progressives with no links to Moscow whatsoever. Liberals called it a "Red Scare."

As we shall see in the next chapter, since the end of the Soviet Union, the opening of KGB archives, and the 1995 publication of American intelligence decryptions known as the Venona files, the identities of Americans spying for Moscow in the 1940s are now known. The decades-long controversy over, for instance, the most famous suspected spy, Alger Hiss, should be happily ended. In fact, it should never have pumped into the *Kultursmog* more than a passing puff of contaminant. There was an abundance of evidence against Hiss long ago, and by the late 1990s his guilt had been proved beyond reasonable doubt. Yet up there in the *smog*, Alger remains innocent and actually revered, which, given the thickness of the *smog*, is, perhaps, understandable. Those who live in its haze cannot be expected to recognize another point of view, much less reality.

Months after the Venona files were made public, former senator George McGovern, a lifelong denizen of the *Kultursmog*, blithely passed along the resilient falsehood, asseverating: "I've always believed that Hiss was a victim of the 'Red Scare,' and Nixon's political rapacity."[9] He was addressing a 1996 meeting of the American Historical Association. Utterly unaffected by the new evidence against Hiss, McGovern, the 1972 Democratic presidential candidate, went on to intone to the assembled historians the obligatory indignation, "It is a national outrage that this essentially decent man went to prison as a consequence of the demagoguery of Nixon and the ignominious House Committee on Un-American Activities."[10] Here you see the *smog* in the making. A famous Liberal repeats a choice falsehood, which he will apparently be repeating unto death. He repeats it to an influential audience likely to spread the tainted word. Finally, there is that "outrage," so indispensable to the Angry Liberal's growing irritability.

The recirculating falsehoods give those who repeat them a sense of superiority, occasionally a sense of invulnerability that can end disastrously. Such disaster befell a besmogged mind a year after McGovern spoke at the American Historical Association meeting, and well after intelligent observers had digested the Venona revelations about Hiss—at least intelligent observers who were unbefogged by the *Kultursmog*. One Sunday morning on *Meet the Press*, President Bill Clinton's national security adviser, Anthony Lake, expressed doubt about Hiss's espionage activity, despite being at the time the president's nominee to head the CIA, our premier spying agency.[11] Admittedly

Meet the Press is comfortable *Kultursmog* terrain, but not all its viewers are sozzled by Liberal contaminants. There followed a dreadful outcry against having a Hiss apologist in such a sensitive post. Soon a bewildered Lake was forced to withdraw his nomination, and you can be sure he was very angry. "What the hell was that all about?" one can imagine his asking. And in 1997 Liberals did not even have Sarah Palin to blame the outrage on.

Other instances of what Piereson calls the "Liberal understanding of events" enlarging the *Kultursmog* are the inveterate repetition of claims (1) that Al Gore won Florida's presidential vote in 2000, (2) that George W. Bush lied about Saddam Hussein possessing weapons of mass destruction, (3) that supply-side economics is a failure, and I should not snicker but (4) that President Clinton was the victim of a "vast right-wing conspiracy,"[12] rather than that constant disturbance in his pants. All these whoppers persist despite an abundance of evidence to the contrary. Their monotonous repetition leaves the *smog*'s victims quite helplessly brainwashed.

No credible examination of the Florida vote count has supported the idea that Gore won. In fact, on November 12, 2001, the *Washington Post* reported that, after examining the Florida returns with a consortium of nine other news agencies, "in all likelihood, George W. Bush still would have won Florida and the presidency last year if either of two limited recounts—one requested by Al Gore, the other ordered by the Florida Supreme Court—had been completed."[13] Earlier in the year, the *Miami Herald* and *USA*

Today concluded that Bush's lead would have actually increased by 537 votes had the Florida Supreme Court's ordered recount continued.[14] Nevertheless, Liberals dutifully recirculate this falsehood throughout the *Kultursmog*'s fetid atmosphere.

Sometimes they do so as officials of the United States government. Nine years after the 2000 election, Hillary Clinton, then secretary of state, addressed an audience in Nigeria and compared the 2000 Florida election to the stolen elections that are the norm in that corrupt country. She even named the election's fixer: "As you may remember, in 2000 our presidential election came down to one state where the brother of one of the men running for president was governor of the state. So we have our problems too."[15]

As for the *Kultursmog*'s repeated falsehood that Bush lied in telling Congress and the American people that Saddam Hussein had weapons of mass destruction, it was clearly not a lie but a mistaken belief. Concocted by Hussein himself, this mistaken belief was held by intelligence agencies throughout the world. If Bush were lying, he would have to be about as stupid as Hussein, for his lie would be exposed soon after the American army subdued Iraq and found no weapons of mass destruction. Today we know that even Hussein's military commanders believed his boasts about possessing these weapons. Since Hussein's fall, scores of articles and books have proved that Bush was operating on mistaken intelligence, not on the hope of deceiving the public. Perhaps the most persuasive book covering the matter is Charles A. Duelfer's *Hide and Seek:*

The Search for Truth in Iraq.[16] In it Duelfer, a respected UN weapons inspector in the 1990s and later head of the Iraq Survey Group, reports that Hussein admitted to his American captors that he had lied to the world about having weapons of mass destruction to intimidate neighboring countries. That lie cooked his goose.

The *Kultursmog*'s repeated falsehood that supply-side economics has been a dud relies mostly on misrepresentation of supply-side's promise. Most of supply-side's leading proponents have *not* promised balanced budgets as Liberals allege, but rather economic growth. Balanced budgets are a matter for Congress to maintain. Supply-siders promised economic growth and increased tax revenues as long as tax rates were restrained. They have been vindicated. Productivity growth more than doubled—from 1 percent annually in the decade prior to the Reagan tax cuts to roughly 2.25 percent annually through the two decades following the cuts.[17] As for tax receipts, despite lower top tax rates, individual income tax receipts increased 296 percent (186 percent after adjustment for inflation) between 1983 and 2008.[18] Additionally, the 1980s and 1990s saw the unemployment rate fall to new lows before the tsunami of new spending in the Bush and Obama years.[19]

Finally, the claim that a "conspiracy" was responsible for President Clinton's impeachment is yet another easily disproved falsehood from the *Kultursmog*, one that demonstrates how intellectually bereft are our times. Boy Clinton brought most of his troubles on himself. Aside from some of his critics' knowing each other, historians have yet to turn up what might commonly be accepted as a conspiracy against the forty-second president. Clinton, of his own volition, entered into an affair with Monica Lewinsky and then lied about it as he has lied about so much else. To believe in what Hillary termed a "vast right-wing conspiracy" is to suffer what the historian Richard Hofstadter called the "paranoid style in American politics,"[20] though Hofstadter mistakenly conceived it as a disorder suffered by conservatives, not Liberals.

Currently, of course, one of the most pervasive falsehoods recirculated throughout the *Kultursmog* is the one that we addressed in chapter 1, the canard that conservatism is on its way out. Doubtless the gruesome judgment is shared by Anthony Lake and by George McGovern. Were he not in heaven, surrounded by archangels, it would be shared by Alger Hiss, too, and all the other victims of the *Kultursmog* for whom this book is meant as therapy.

The *Kultursmog*'s second modus operandi is its practice of neglecting or misrepresenting conservatives. Those of us committed to cleaning up the *Kultursmog*—call us intellectual environmentalists—have observed these practices for years, but there is little we can do about them. We have no influence in the awarding of Pulitzer Prizes or any of the other nationally recognized awards that confer status on members of the intelligentsia. We have not even been able to persuade the various Pulitzer committees to desist from giving their awards to plagiarists or to rescind the Pulitzers once a plagiarist is exposed. The career of Bill Buckley is instructive. Lasting some five decades, it involved so many journalistic achievements that at his death the *New York Sun* duly proclaimed Bill "one of the 20ᵗʰ century's greatest journalists."[21] Yet the *Sun* was not part of the *Kultursmog*. It was an organ of the conservative movement's now expanding counterculture. As for the *Kultursmog*, its organs and agents conferred not one major journalistic award or any cultural recognition on him other than a lone Emmy for *Firing Line*, his television series that lasted thirty-three years.

A now-classic inquiry into how the *smog* has neglected or misrepresented conservatives was conducted in the 1990s by Adam Meyerson in the quarterly that he edited for the Heritage Foundation, *Policy Review*.[22] He found that the *smog* had tainted even standard reference books, namely the sixteenth edition of *Bartlett's Familiar Quotations*. In it Liberals' achievements are repeatedly exaggerated, while conservatives are ignored, diminished, and at times misrepresented.

John Kenneth Galbraith, a mediocre celebrity economist, is remembered with eleven quotations, all bespeaking one Liberal intellectual staple or another, most of which now stand revealed as poppycock. Milton Friedman and F. A. Hayek, though winners of the Nobel Prize for economics, account for three and two quotations respectively. Prime minister Margaret Thatcher and Pope John Paul II, two conservatives now generally acknowledged to have been crucial to the peaceful end of the Cold War, are remembered with two quotations each, neither particularly memorable nor suggestive of their enormous achievements. Rock singers

Joni Mitchell and Bruce Springsteen are memorialized with the same number of quotations, and the Rolling Stones have four. A clown figure, Cookie Monster, from the children's TV series *Sesame Street*, is remembered for the line, "Me want cookie!" and a minor novelist, Erica Jong, is remembered for her metaphysical confection, "the zipless f—."

As for presidents, John F. Kennedy Jr. gets twenty-eight entries; Franklin Delano Roosevelt, thirty-five; and Ronald Reagan, three. Though Reagan was the first president to finish two terms since Dwight Eisenhower, he gets no more recognition than Zachary Taylor, whose presidency lasted sixteen months, and Gerald Ford, whose presidency lasted two years and five months. Reagan's historic 1984 "Boys of Pointe du Hoc" speech delivered on the fortieth anniversary of D-day is ignored, as is his 1987 plea delivered at the Brandenburg Gate: "Mr. Gorbachev, open this gate! Mr. Gorbachev, tear down this wall!" The wall came down, and the Soviet Union collapsed, but the editor of *Bartlett's* perceived nothing in Reagan's speech worth remembering. Ignored also in this famous reference book is Reagan's prescient 1981 prediction of Communism's demise as a "bizarre chapter in human history whose last pages are even now being written." In the *Kultursmog* Reagan remained a minor figure with fewer quotations than the Rolling Stones. What quotations the sixteenth edition of *Bartlett's* does produce depict Reagan as precisely the kind of conservative that Liberals envisage, a fatuous materialist.

When the *Philadelphia Inquirer* interviewed Justin Kaplan, the volume's editor, about his treatment of Reagan,

Kaplan seethed, "I'm not going to disguise the fact that I despise Ronald Reagan"—Liberal outrage! Whereupon he rationalized that the president, then known as "the Great Communicator," "could not be described as a memorable phrase maker" but rather as "an actor masquerading as a leader."[23] Interviewed for this book on whether the next edition of *Bartlett's* published in 2002 is freer of the *smog*, Meyerson reported, "It's not much better."[24] Reagan now has six quotations, including his exhortations at the Brandenburg Gate, but not the others mentioned above. However, he now shares space with the Reverend Jesse Jackson; the poet laureate of New Jersey, Amiri Baraka; and Gloria Steinem.

The effect of the *Kultursmog's* steady drizzle of falsehoods, neglect, and misrepresentation on a conservative personage has been demonstrable and is often quantifiable. Ronald Reagan left office with an approval rating of some 68 percent—the highest of any outgoing president since World War II.[25] In the years that followed he did nothing to dishonor himself. No new evidence of high crimes or misdemeanors turned up. Yet the steady repetition of the *Kultursmog's* falsehoods about him and its neglect in acknowledging his achievements had its corrosive effect on that 68 percent approval rating. When he spoke at the GOP convention to support George H. W. Bush's reelection, a New York Times/CBS News Poll claimed that only 37 percent of the citizenry held a favorable view of the Reagan presidency.[26] Sometimes the *Kultursmog's* corrosion works on a conservative's reputation much faster.

After Clarence Thomas survived Anita Hill's lurid charges during his nomination hearings, the public sided with him by two to one. A year later the public's opinion shifted to side with Hill by 44 percent to 34 percent.[27] No new evidence had entered the controversy, just the steady *drip*, *drip* of the *Kultursmog's* falsehoods, neglect, and misrepresentations against the new Supreme Court justice.

Just as *the Kultursmog*'s repeated falsehoods need no supporting evidence, its repeated misrepresentations need no supporting evidence. At the *American Spectator* I personally experienced this corrosive process after nearly a decade of happily publishing investigative journalism into the Clintons' derring-do. The stories were all accurate and to this day have not been proved inaccurate. Yet at some point in the 1990s, it became commonplace in the *Kultursmog* to refer to them as untruthful even though other publications had followed up with similar stories, a series of corroborations never mentioned at the time or in later histories of the period—again, *Kultursmog* neglect.

Our first Troopergate story in December 1993 exposed Clinton's transformation of his Arkansas state trooper security detail into a team of pimps, essential for his peculiar sexual hygiene. The *Spectator* broke the story, but shortly thereafter the *Los Angles Times* published similar revelations—a corroboration soon lost in the *smog*. Today the Troopergate stories are almost exclusively attributed to the *Spectator*, with the *Los Angeles Times* rarely mentioned and the implication being that Troopergate was without merit. All of this, notwithstanding the fact that the original

story in the *Spectator* was the source of the sexual harass-
ment suit that led to Clinton's impeachment. Moreover
Monica Lewinsky's testimony contained revelations about
Clinton's odd sexual beliefs and practices that had
appeared five years earlier in the Arkansas troopers' stories
in the *Spectator*.

Over the next few years, the *Spectator* proceeded to
publish stories of the Clintons' political and financial
shenanigans that were often groundbreaking. Not one has
ever been disproved. We even puckishly published an exposé
of the Boy President's habitual cheating on the golf course.
It was completely accurate and, as with the first Troopergate
piece, followed up with corroboration in the mainstream
media, for instance, stories from Gannett News Service.
"President Clinton has developed the mulligan into a fine
art," wrote journalist John Omicinski for Gannett in August
1997. "Apparently Clinton's Zeitgeist tells him that if he
thinks he shot 79, then he shot 79. Call it Zen golf."[28] More
confirmation came later in an entire book by Don van Natta,
First Off the Tee.[29]

As I say, no one has refuted these stories. Yet, the
Kultursmog's contaminants remain encrusted on the
Spectator and continue to taint our credibility in news-
papers and periodicals and, of course, on the Internet. Even
serious historical studies have begun spreading the pollution. The *Spectator* stories were "a series of half-truthful
articles about the Clintons' sex life and dodgy business
dealings," according to the authors of *The Right Nation:
Conservative Power in America*, published in 2004.[30] The

stories were "mostly untrue," according to Steven M. Gillon's *The Pact: Bill Clinton, Newt Gingrich, and the Rivalry That Defined a Generation*, published in 2008.[31] Neither book offered evidence of the *Spectator*'s inaccuracies, much less an offending quotation. Their claims will probably circulate through the *smog* for as long as the claims about Alger Hiss's innocence circulate, which is to say until the *smog* dissipates—unto eternity.

In my role as intellectual environmentalist, I wonder at times as to precisely how preposterous an unsubstantiated claim has to be to be ignored by the *Kultursmog*. For instance, the Clintons' factotum, Terry McAuliffe, in his memoir claims that the *Spectator* published articles alleging that Clinton "ordered the murder of political opponents.[32] Will that unsubstantiated claim endure in the *smog*? As with the earlier misrepresentations, McAuliffe failed to cite the publication dates of these shocking pieces. I very politely initiated a correspondence with him, inquiring as to the whereabouts of these articles in the magazine, which, not incidentally, I edit. Full of arrogance, he BS'd back and forth to me, but always without any evidence whatsoever. He never admitted he was wrong but also never provided the necessary citations to substantiate his charge. Eventually our epistolary relationship had to come to a halt. I published the idiotic correspondence in our December 2008/January 2009 issue. I have not heard from him since.

Even easily refutable claims take on a life of their own in the *Kultursmog*. *The Pact*, for instance, written by Gillon, a serious historian, passed on the risible claim first made by another historian, Nigel Hamilton, in his biography, *Bill Clinton: An American Journey*. According to Hamilton, I attended Georgetown University with Clinton, a revelation that should have stirred the curiosity of journalists. After all, by the time these books came out, the editor in chief of the *American Spectator* had become somewhat of a figure in the Clinton scandals. The revelation that I went to college with Bill deserved at least an inquiry. Was there some untoward campus event all those years ago that transformed me into my old classmate's nemesis? The telephone never rang. No journalist has ever called—again, *Kultursmog* neglect. (For the record, and as I have already stated, I attended Indiana University.)

By the 1990s hopes were improving for the establishment of a conservative counterculture that might expose the falsehoods and misrepresentations of the *Kultursmog* and recognize conservatives and their work. Conservatism had grown into a mass movement—in fact, a larger mass movement than Liberalism. Noting the development, Rupert Murdoch founded Fox News, which claimed with some legitimacy to be "fair and balanced," but as a business proposition catered to a large and self-consciously conservative audience. That, in the ensuing years, Fox News became the country's largest cable network confirmed Murdoch's fine business instincts. Fox's success also reinforces my contention in this book that conservatism in America is more popular than Liberalism and in no danger of dying.

Also in the realm of broadcast media, conservative talk radio became a medium for circulating conservative ideas with huge national shows modeled on that of talk show superstar Rush Limbaugh, and with local shows in practically every city in the country. Curiously, even when championed by Liberal leaders of the magnitude of Al Gore, efforts to establish a Liberal alternative to conservative talk radio proved futile. Along with the broadcast media, the promising conservative counterculture included its intellectual journals that had sustained conservatism in the years of Goldwater and Reagan, for instance, *National Review*, *Human Events*, *Commentary*, *American Spectator*, and the *Weekly Standard*. All experienced vigorous growth in the 1990s. There were also specialized intellectual quarterlies, such as the *Public Interest* and *Policy Review*, influencing the public discourse. Competing with the *Kultursmog*'s *New York Times* and *Washington Post* were the venerable *Wall Street Journal* and a surprisingly durable *Washington Times*.

Yet the *Kultursmog*'s ability to diminish and misrepresent conservatives remained formidable, for the Liberals' angers were, as we have seen, intensifying. The most popular explanation for this intensifying anger is that Liberalism in the media and in politics never expected the strong conservative challenge. During the forty years of Democratic congressional dominance, Republican senators and congressmen were no threat to the Democrats, and both sides were more sedate and even courtly than today. Another explanation for the Liberals' anger is that they come from the 1960s generation, whose left was and has remained enormously angry, having experienced street protests, campus takeovers, and the famous "Days of Rage" during its troubled youth, emotional indulgences that the 1960s left-wing generation never quite grew out of. Think about it. On Nancy Pelosi a scowl looks natural. She has been wearing it for years. Finally, there is Sunstein's explanation. Like-minded people congregating with one another become more extreme and outraged. Whatever the cause—and probably all three are at work—the Liberals' *Kultursmog* has been difficult for the conservative counterculture to aerate or to oppose. By the presidency of George W. Bush, the *smog*'s interpretation of the news had moved from the merely tendentious to the arrantly propagandistic.

The *Kultursmog* has damaged the conservative movement in three ways. First the *smog* has denied conservatives the status they have merited. Frequently their achievements go unmentioned, their books ignored in the mainstream media, and their other achievements distorted, diminished, or ignored. Serious students of history might know that Clarence Thomas never harassed Anita Hill, but how are ordinary Americans constantly being assailed by the repetitions of the *smog* to know? Erudite readers might know that Thomas has produced one of the finest memoirs written by a public figure from his generation, but how is an ordinary person to know? According to the *Washington Post*'s report on the book's publication, headlined, "Justice Thomas Lashes Out in Memoir," Thomas "settles scores in an angry and vivid forthcoming memoir, scathingly condemning the media, the Democratic senators who opposed his nomination to the Supreme Court, and the 'mob' of liberal elites and activist groups that he says desecrated his life."[33] That was only the *Post*'s first sentence! Incidentally, two of the three writers contributing to the ambush had written a highly critical biography of Thomas, though the obvious conflict of interest was never revealed in their tirade.[34] *The New York Times* review was equally contemptuous and misleading.[35] For that matter, how is an ordinary reader to know that the *Spectator*'s articles on Clinton were not "mostly untrue," as *The Pact* reports, or "half-truthful," as *The Right Nation* puts it?

If the *smog* can taint conservative organizations and leaders, it can hinder ongoing organization within the movement. Such groups as the National Rifle Association (NRA) and the Federalist Society, the conservatives' foremost organization of lawyers, law students, faculty members, and others interested in the law, are under constant assault from the *smog*. The propaganda swirling about these two groups presents the NRA as a group of gun nuts and the Federalist Society as secretive and extremist, though in pursuit of precisely *what* it is never revealed. Liberals can be very vague about the precise nature of the Conservative Conspiracy.

Actually the NRA is a perfectly responsible group interested in much more than firearms. The NRA's interests include hunting and fishing, environmental protection (the hunters and anglers call it "habitat protection"), the Bill of Rights, and other civic matters. The Federalist

Society is interested in understanding the principles of our constitutional government and how it has preserved liberty and the rule of law for over two centuries. To taint such groups is to make it difficult for them to grow and to carry on their activities. That they do continue to grow is more evidence of conservatism's vitality despite its critics' grim diagnoses and obituaries.

The second malign effect the *Kultursmog* has had on the conservative movement and on the ability of the conservative counterculture to counter the *smog* is that it has exaggerated every conservative problem. This we have seen with the post-2008 election's repeated falsehood that conservatism is suffering rigor mortis. Moreover, the *smog* exaggerates every conservative's least misstep. Can you think of one conservative alive at the end of the Bush administration in 2008 who was widely admired in the press? Senator Edward Kennedy survives the death of Mary Jo Kopechne and carousals that end in rape and scandal but dies an American immortal, "the Lion of the Senate." The Reverend Jesse Jackson survives being caught in anti-Semitic utterances, financial scandals, and forget not his clownish arrival at the White House to counsel President Clinton on his marital infidelities with a pregnant mistress on his arm.[36] He remains a leading civil rights leader. The Boy President is caught in unprecedented campaign finance violations, lying to a prosecutor and to the American people. He is impeached and emerges as what the press calls "a rock star." Congressman Barney Frank is caught maintaining a homosexual bordello in his Washington residence and lives to be a leader in the Congress. Vice President Biden is an admitted plagiarist. Senator John Kerry is an exposed résumé cheat. The list of Liberal eminences surviving scandals is long, but any list of blameless conservatives is presented in the *Kultursmog* as a list of dubious figures. Grover Norquist, the ubiquitous head of Americans for Tax Reform, evokes tut-tuts. So does Dick Armey, former House Majority Leader and now a leading activist in the conservatives' road to recovery, and all conservative talk show hosts. Yet all are for the most part blameless save for their devotion to causes disapproved of in the *smog*.

The third malign effect that the *Kultursmog* has had on conservatives is the most serious because it has caused the most serious problem facing the conservative movement, namely, its difficulty in pulling together. As Adam Meyerson observed looking back on the conservatives in the last years of the Bush administration, "It's like they're in a cocoon. They don't talk much to each other."[37] The *Kultursmog* has successfully marginalized the conservatives and their organizations, creating debilitating rivalries. The marginalization worsened throughout the Bush years, and the rivalries became more intense. The presence of the conservative counterculture gave the conservatives a platform from which to make reputations for themselves, but that only seemed to intensify the careerism.

The *Kultursmog*'s marginalization of conservatives began in the Reagan years after a fleeting if tepid hospitality was shown to the conservatives and neoconservatives in the 1970s. That the marginalization was possible is an indication of the *Kultursmog*'s powerful influence. The president of the United States was a movement conservative. He had brought like-minded conservatives with him into government. He was popular with the American people, but still the *smog* marginalized his fellow conservatives. Unlike FDR's New Order (the term was popularized by the historian Arthur M. Schlesinger Jr.), Reagan's New Order would not be changing the political culture much. Here is but another demonstration of my thesis about the conservatives' limited appetite for politics. Whereas the Liberals have an insatiable political libido, the conservatives' political libido is that of a Victorian. The consequence is that the Liberal gets into political difficulties because of excess; the conservative usually gets into political trouble because of acts of omission. Even as politically astute a conservative as President Reagan failed to insinuate conservatism into American culture. In fact, as I observed at the end of his administration in *The Conservative Crack-Up*, he hardly tried.

It is difficult to demonstrate an act of omission, but the Liberals' record of moving back and forth from politics to culture should provide some illumination for future conservative leaders. President Franklin Roosevelt and his New Dealers did it throughout the 1930s and 1940s, creating the first signs of *Kultursmog*. With Roosevelt's election, the nascent New Dealers left their posts in the universities, on Wall Street, and at such intellectual reviews as the *Nation* and the *New Republic*, to enter the administration. New Dealers such as Robert Sherwood and Archibald MacLeish were active both in government and in culture. Sherwood, as a playwright, brought broad New Deal themes to the stage with such dramas as *The Petrified Forest* (1934), *Idiot's Delight* (1936), and *There Shall Be No Night* (1940). *Idiot's Delight* won a Pulitzer Prize. The poet MacLeish grew steadily as a cultural figure in the 1930s, and he won a Pulitzer Prize for his narrative poem, *Conquistador*. Both wrote speeches for the president. Both held significant positions in government, Sherwood as special assistant to the secretary of the Navy, MacLeish as librarian of Congress and assistant secretary of state. No migrations between the realms of politics and culture like this took place during the Reagan years. The cultural world of the 1980s would not allow it, and the Reaganites would not attempt it. Composers, most notably Aaron Copland and Virgil Thomson, gained stature, frequently composing music reflecting popular themes of New Deal lore, and Thomson composed music for documentaries celebrating New Deal projects, *The River* and *The Plough That Broke the Plains*. Nothing like this took place with the conservatives during the Reagan years.

The same synergy between politics and culture went on during the New Frontier too. The professoriate came into the Kennedy administration led by Schlesinger and John Kenneth Galbraith. The New Frontier eagerly recruited artists, scholars, and writers for government service. More than fifty writers, painters, and composers were invited to JFK's inauguration. "What a joy," exulted John Steinbeck, "that literacy is no longer *prima facie* evidence of treason."[38] From a Caribbean safe house on the island of Saint

Lucia, Archibald MacLeish sent his appreciation to the newly elected president after hearing his inaugural address on an "uncertain short-wave radio." "It left me proud and hopeful to be an American—" he said, "something I have not felt for almost twenty years. I owe you and send you my deepest gratitude."[39] Obviously, by 1960 the *Kultursmog* was thickening, and remember what I have said about the values of Liberalism being petrified in time. Is there not something in MacLeish's sycophantic drivel strongly reminiscent of the drivel we heard when the Prophet Obama was inaugurated?

In the New Frontier, you had the same movement of writers from speechwriting to high government posts that you had in the New Deal. For instance, the distinguished White House speechwriter Richard Goodwin moved on to policymaking in the State Department.

Unfortunately, the experience of two successful Democratic presidencies in the realm of cultural politics taught the Republican administration of the 1980s nothing at all. No conservative literary figure was invited to any position in the government, not Tom Wolfe or Walker Percy or even the popular novelist Tom Clancy. Let us face the facts squarely. Liberals have a more expansive view of politics than conservatives. It makes them politically more effective, at least when their overactive political libidos are in check. They affix themselves to politics and to culture and revise both where they can. They understand that politics is more than a set of policies. In democracy it is the promotion of a culture, a web of principles, sympathies, manners, all the fruits of intellect. The conservatives' conception of politics is more limited.

Consequently the *Kultursmog*'s marginalization of the conservatives continued during the presidency of George W. Bush as their petty rivalries continued to intensify. This explains how what was once a tight-knit political movement fissured from the careerism of some of the conservative personalities and the opportunism of the Reformed Conservatives and their variants. Reviewing the opportunists and their sly disparagement of genuine conservatives, Herb London, currently head of the distinguished conservative think tank, the Hudson Institute, has remarked, "These so-called conservatives have a habit of leapfrogging over each other. Their opportunities for advancement in the culture and the media are limited, and in pursuit of the klieg lights they engage in warfare against one another."[40] Clever operators beginning their careers from the conservative side have figured how to acquire celebrity and at least ephemeral advancement by playing to the *smog*'s prejudices and diminishing other conservatives or utterly misrepresenting them. The more unscrupulous have repeated the *smog*'s falsehoods. We saw this earlier with Ross Douthat in his putatively conservative *New York Times* column blithely passing on the *smog*'s falsehoods about Senator Jeff Sessions's "history of racially charged remarks."[41]

Most of the RCs' warnings about conservatism's morbidity in 2008 were simply exploitations of the *Kultursmog*'s repeated falsehood that conservatism was kaput. Christopher Buckley's opportunism began at his father's memorial service, where he trivialized a great man. The opportunism got more blatant when he joined in the hysteria over Sarah Palin and endorsed Barack Obama as a politician too intelligent to attempt "traditional left-politics" once elected president.[42] Of course, it reached a culmination with the revelations about his family in his appalling memoir. All this helped Buckley maintain celebrity in the *Kultursmog*, but it contributed enormously to the *smog*'s claim that conservatism was dying. What is more, it diminished the reputation of a great conservative leader, his father. In the *smog*, Christopher's depiction of his father being an irritable, self-absorbed, disengaged parent will never die, at least until the *Kultursmog* dies.

This diminishment of other conservatives and of conservative organizations by these self-marketing opportunists is an example of what social anthropologists studying other marginalized people call "crab antics." Studying upward mobility among marginalized populations in the Caribbean, anthropologists have noted that many act like crabs at the bottom of a bucket. When it is tipped, the crabs scramble to leap over one another, or as London says, leapfrog over one another. Some pull others back. The crabs at the top must always evade their rivals' outstretched claws or fall back into the bucket. As I have said, I do not expect the beauteous Sarah to get out of the bucket, but the sight of her down there in a heap with the likes of Christopher Buckley, Douthat, and David Frum could be an amusing, if slightly lewd, spectacle.

What is going to happen in the *Kultursmog*? Will it destroy the planet? Will it cause deformity in fetuses and crop damage in the Heartland? Will it simply make independent thought impossible and independent thinkers invisible, forever consigned to a conservative counterculture that is always to be marginal? Well, as the *smog* continues to lose touch with terra firma, I think catastrophe will be averted. The *Kultursmog* will eventually weaken and blow out to sea. From the grassroots rebellion against the Obama administration's threats to freedom and stupefying profligacy, we can see that huge numbers of Americans still cherish their freedom and the capitalist ladder to riches. They have resisted the *smog*. Increasingly they rely on the growing conservative counterculture.

Independent thought is thriving on the Internet. New Internet publications are replacing the old smokestacks of the *smog*, and often exposing them for the bunk pushers that they are. Recall how the bloggers exposed the obvious phoniness of the documents that Dan Rather thought would discredit George W. Bush in 2004 and send him into early retirement. In the *smog* Rather remains a "truth teller," but the real truth is that he is a has-been, a discredited ex-anchorman. Only a pathetico hopelessly sozzled in the *Kultursmog* believes those forged documents to be anything but the evidence of a hoax.

Or recall how the Web sites kept the drumbeat going against Van Jones, the Obama administration environmental czar who had *become* a Communist in the 1990s—not the 1890s, the 1990s!—and signed a 2004 petition charging "that the people within the administration may indeed have allowed 9/11 to happen, perhaps as a pretext to war."[43] They beat their tom-toms for well over a week before Jones was forced to resign. During that period network news carried not one story. The *New York Times* was equally mum. *The Los Angeles Times*'s one story chided Fox News for reporting the scandal in the first place. Through it all the *Washington Post* maintained a gentlemanly silence, reporting the story only on the day that Jones resigned. Yet these aging organs of the *Kultursmog* were not necessary. New media sounded the tocsin.

A few days later, word began to be carried on the Internet about a delightful sting operation perpetrated by two rosy-cheeked young conservatives (ages twenty-five and twenty) who presented themselves at ACORN (Association of Community Organizations for Reform Now) offices across the country, claiming to be entrepreneurs in the sex trade and seeking practical tips on how to get a home loan for their brothel. They sought counsel on how to cheat the IRS and launder money. ACORN, a left-wing "community action" outfit, had long been the target of law enforcement agencies for various suspected felonies, most notably voter fraud and misuse of government money. Mainstream media rarely covered the investigations. Now young conservative investigative journalists had ACORN employees on tape, counseling them on the launch of their fictitious brothel. The ACORN counselors even informed the conservative youths on how to camouflage the use of underage Central American prostitutes. One ACORN counselor advised on how the Central Americans could be used to extract child tax credits from the government. Once again the news organs of the *Kultursmog* ignored the story. But the conservative counterculture picked it up, led by Andrew Breitbart on the Internet and Fox News on television. Soon the *smog* was thwarted, and ACORN was exposed for the criminal enterprise that it had become. All such incidents point to the rising power of the conservative counterculture. Increasingly the *Kultursmog* will be but a minor irritant, like a skunk temporarily perfuming an evening breeze.

The *Kultursmog*'s dependence on Liberalism ensures its dismal prospects, for Liberalism's future is as dubious as I have adumbrated throughout this book. Someday the culture of the country will be completely free of the *smog*'s pollutions. Angry Liberals preaching an economic program that failed in China and in India a generation ago are not likely to replace the conservatives' economic policies that are now making present-day China and India prosperous. Angry Liberals preaching not just Big Government but in Obama's era Behemoth Government are not going to quiet the Tea Party Americans and whatever variants of the freedom-loving Yanks come next. A new coalition of senior citizens (worried about their health care) and young voters (worried about entitlements) seems to be exquisitely apprehensive over the Obama excesses. The overactive Liberal political libido has done it again: repulsed the *popolo minuto*.

Yet if the conservative counterculture is to vanquish the *smog*, it has to start acting like a culture. There has to be intellectual activity *shared* among the conservative activists, personalities, and writers. The movement's members have to desist from their solipsistic leapfrogging and do what I urged upon Bill Buckley back in 1986, to wit, take an interest in each other's work—at least when it is interesting. Moreover they have to assess each other and each other's work with a clear sense unclouded by the *smog*'s vapors. "Many conservatives try to establish their bona fides by attacking other conservatives," says Jim Piereson, "which will make them well liked by Liberals, which is the point."[44] A most egregious example of this behavior was a slanderous attack on the integrity of Grover Norquist by Tucker Carlson, the ambitious conservative journalist whose taxonomy in the conservative movement has been labeled "mini-con"—with the emphasis on "con." Indicative of the personal advancement that he was up to, he performed his poorly sourced hatchet job in the Liberal *New Republic*,[45] though his name was at the time on the masthead of the *Weekly Standard*. It was a characteristically overwrought barrage of deceitful charges, the key deceit being that Carlson's father had a personal interest in discrediting Norquist. The hatchet job even roused the ire of the *Washington Post*'s media critic, Howard Kurtz, who called Carlson's piece "a black mark" on his career.[46] Nonetheless, it served its purpose, ensuring that Carlson remain a speck in the *smog*.

There was a day when conservatives did not remark on other conservatives invidiously to curry favor with Liberals. In the 1960s and 1970s, the leading conservative syndicated columnists referred to each other in their writings as a means of contributing to the public discourse and informing their readers of developments in intellectual and political life. Sometimes they joked. Sometimes they picked up on a colleague's idea or turn of phrase. Sometimes they were in agreement, sometimes in disagreement. The point is that they maintained a dialogue for the purpose of informing their readers. Four who did so with some frequency were John Chamberlain, James Jackson Kilpatrick, Russell Kirk, and Buckley. They appeared together in public forums and on television shows. They were not competing with one another but interacting intelligently. At some point such collegiality broke down, to be replaced by today's rat race of egotists.

Yet there is a model for how the conservative counterculture can resume this kind of give-and-take. It is the dialogue maintained by the big three in conservative talk radio: Rush Limbaugh, Sean Hannity, and Mark Levin. They mention one another not with the intention of diminishing each other but with the intention of carrying on a dialogue for the enlightenment of their listeners. Sometimes they are critical of one another. More often they are complimentary. After all, they are usually in agreement. That is to be expected of people in the same movement. And these three conservative personalities are very much aware that they are in the same movement, hoping to advance personal liberty and American conservative values. Always they are invigorating conservatism at the popular level.

Conservative talk radio also embraces the opposite of these conservative leaders, for instance Joe Scarborough, the ex-congressman, an RC for the airwaves. As it turns out, he has exiguous background in the ideas of the movement. He was a Florida lawyer before running for Congress in 1994 on what he himself implies was a whim. After leaving Congress in 2001, he found his way to MSNBC and a cable show where he specializes in calling himself conservative while managing to be on both sides of most issues or sniping at genuine conservatives. Through the years he has rarely manifested an interest in much beyond his own self-promotion. Whereas Limbaugh, Hannity, and Levin sell conservative principles, Scarborough uses conservative principles to sell himself. He is not a leader in the movement but the rider on it. Like the mini-cons and the RCs, he is adept in self-advancement and in diminishing conservatives. Limbaugh, Hannity, and Levin are examples of what the conservative writers and policy experts ought to be: colleagues in a cause.

FORGED
IN FLAMES

The Battles That Gave American
Conservatism Its Definition

What, then, is conservatism? Or to be precise, what is modern American conservatism, the conservatism that, when it made its appearance in the early 1950s, was called the New Conservatism and for the past fifty or sixty years has been known as "movement conservatism" by those of us who have espoused it?

From the 1950s on, the question was often asked of William F. Buckley, Jr. when he lectured across the country as modern conservatism's first great herald. The definition Bill favored and delivered with arch demeanor was formulated by one of the movement's founding theorists, the University of Chicago's Richard M. Weaver, author of a 1948 book that contemporary conservatives still quote, *Ideas Have Consequences*. To attentive audiences Bill would explain that conservatism is "the paradigm of essences towards which the phenomenology of the world is in continuing approximation." Weaver might have been in earnest when he laid down that formulation. Bill was not. Bringing to conservatism puckish wit and a sure sense for the dramatic, Bill was not only conservatism's first herald but also its first personality. Weaver's definition was Bill's idea of a joke, a sophisticated joke that might at once amuse and instruct audiences throughout the first half of Bill's public life, before the Zeitgeist changed, and the culture dumbed down.

Such jokes worked for Bill into the 1980s. For much of that time, the growing number of Americans who considered themselves forthrightly conservative also considered themselves somehow elevated above the mass of ordinary Americans, particularly above their opponents, the Liberals. Imagine, however, if one of contemporary conservatism's personalities attempted Bill's joke today, employing Professor Weaver's "paradigm of essences." Audience members might literally run off the road, for as conservatism has grown from its select cadre of 1950s sophisticates to the vast market share that it commands today, it has replaced stale and moribund rock and roll on hundreds of radio stations. Radio audiences have become an important element in conservatism's political base, as important to that base as African Americans are to Liberalism's base. How African Americans came to support the Democratic Party is pretty well understood. How radio audiences came to support conservatism remains mysterious. Is it possible that rock and roll's decline left dispirited Beatles and Elvis fans longing for Rush Limbaugh? All we know for sure is that Liberal radio personalities in the last decade of the twentieth century and the first decade of the twenty-first century could never muster much of an audience; but conservatives did, even in areas dominated by Liberal politics, for instance, the Boston radio audience where conservative Howard Carr dominates the airwaves. For these Massachusetts listeners, and conservative talk radio audiences across the country, a broader definition of conservatism is needed.

Actually, even in the 1950s a broader definition or at least a more easily comprehensible definition of conservatism was needed. Even in the 1950s the conservative movement had a wider base than merely the sophisticated, self-conscious New Conservatives around Buckley, *National Review*, and the growing number of intellectual and political organizations, such as the Intercollegiate Studies Institute, the Young Americans for Freedom, and the American Conservative Union. In the immediate aftermath of World War II and the New Deal, Americans were becoming restless. Some were uncomfortable with the big government projects of the New Deal—"collectivism" as they referred to it disparagingly. Others were apprehensive about Communism's apparent replacement of Nazism as a threat to American and to Western values. They, too, were often, though not always, critical of the New Deal, some blaming it for the expansion of Communism in China and throughout Eastern Europe, behind what Winston Churchill called "the Iron Curtain." Finally there were Americans who beheld all this recent tumult and worried that traditional American values—the values of the West—were in danger of being deracinated forever.

These three groups composed the first constituent elements of modern conservatism, the advocates of limited government, the anti-Communists, and the traditionalists. Most of the postwar conservatives shared membership in all three groups. However, some identified with only one or two of the groups. That created tensions within the New Conservatism, giving rise to early premonitions of a conservative crack-up. Nevertheless, the New Conservatism continued to grow, eventually taking aboard disaffected Liberals (the neoconservatives) and others. The evolution makes the formulation of our definition of modern conservatism tricky, but give me time, a few more pages, a small bucket more ink.

In the early days of conservatism, there were other definitions offered for the New Conservatism. The most influential was concocted by one of the New Conservatism's most famous critics, Arthur M. Schlesinger Jr. The son of a distinguished historian, Schlesinger himself became a distinguished historian, and for over half a century he would be one of Liberalism's supreme intellectual figures in part because of his gift for dry aphorism. In a famous 1955 article in *Reporter* magazine, he sniffed that the New Conservatism was "the ethical afterglow of feudalism" and "the politics of nostalgia."[1] The historian's gibes were inspired by the New Conservatives' revival of eighteenth-century British statesman and political thinker Edmund Burke.

The French Revolution's most famous critic, and one whose criticism of that revolution would serve as a rebuttal to all the political ideologues to follow, Burke was toppled from his late-eighteenth-century intellectual dominance and exiled to temporary oblivion by the international left—at least until the New Conservatives grew influential. Burke's theorizing on history's organic growth and his protest against the Enlightenment's enthronement of reason made him inimical to radicals and to twentieth-century progressives. Of course, the New Conservatives thought he was right on both counts, hence their admiration. From the shambles of Nazism and Communism they looked back on him as a prophet who had long before perceived reason's limits in governance. The monstrous projects of the Nazis and the Communists would not have surprised Burke. By the early 1970s the conservatives were also becoming increasingly aware of the "unintended consequences" of Great Societies. That was an awareness provided by their latest recruits, the neoconservatives, who made the term, *unintended consequences*, a watchword for critics of government overreach.

With his gibes about "feudalism" and "nostalgia," Schlesinger was responding with a burlesque of Burke's thought. The historian was also segregating the New Conservatives from modern political life, making them out to be "reactionaries," a slur against them that endures to this day, at least among Liberals who have failed to notice that by the 1990s it was they themselves who had become the reactionaries. By then the conservative Reagan administration had, with policies the Liberals abhorred, brought unparalleled prosperity and security to the country.

Schlesinger seemed to admit his exaggeration elsewhere in his *Reporter* article when he noted the "non-feudal, nonaristocratic, dynamic, progressive business society of the United States" in postwar America.[2] The New Conservatives were aware of this too. Except for the most melancholy traditionalists, the conservatives were as at home in modern nonaristocratic commercial America as was Schlesinger—probably more so. They were equally innocent of charges of feudalism. As the American Constitution was their political blueprint and laissez-faire their way of life, Schlesinger's gibes were flagrant misrepresentations of them. As we have seen, the misrepresentation of conservatives has been an enduring tactic of the culturally dominant Liberals. Thus through the decades the conservatives have been defending themselves in the *Kultursmog* against what in essence was Schlesinger's absurd burlesque. The phenomenon is not unknown to historians; a ridiculous observation becomes a philosophy, then a casus belli. Think of Marxism. Think of feminism.

When the New Conservatism made its appearance in the aftermath of World War II, Liberals were experiencing their first period of doubt since they captured the American political culture during the New Deal. With the Iron Curtain drawn across Europe and all of China recently fallen to the Chinese Communists, the New Deal's diplomacy was almost overnight deemed controversial. Republicans won by a landslide in the 1946 off-year elections and were expected to capture the White House in 1948. Domestic Communism, particularly allegations that Communist spies had served in the Roosevelt administration, became a national issue, one that would envenom American politics for decades.

The confetti that Liberals delight in heaving at each other was temporarily passé, and in fact, from the Liberals' ranks emerged critics who sounded very much like the critics who emerged from the conservatives' ranks in the second Bush administration, the Davidians, the Reformed Conservatives, and the occasional mini-con. Writing in *Harper's* magazine, John Fischer opined that Liberalism was "pretty well used up."[3] Sounding a theme that is often sounded during a movement's time of troubles, Fischer spoke of Liberalism's "intellectual bankruptcy." As the 1952 elections drew near, Joseph C. Harsch in the *Reporter*, then an especially civilized intellectual review, raised the prospect that Liberalism was "obsolete."[4] The magazine continued its funereal rites nine months later after Dwight D. Eisenhower won the White House for the Republicans for the first time in twenty years. Under the headline, "The American Liberal: After the Fair Deal, What?" Eric Goldman, a celebrated Liberal historian, labored for thousands of anxious words.[5]

Perhaps this era of Liberal doubt made the New Conservatism's emergence a bit easier. Whatever the case, the New Conservatism's arrival was met by a peevishness from the Liberals that has never dissipated. Even at the end of the twentieth century, with the Cold War over; prosperity and social justice widespread; and a Democratic president, Bill Clinton, sounding the Reaganite incantation that "the era of big government is over," the Liberals were, as we have seen, very angry. In fact, within a few years, during the last term of George W. Bush, that anger actually became a source of pride, made gloriously manifest in the *Kultursmog*'s much-admired "Angry Liberal."

In the early days of the New Conservatism, one would not have foreseen the eventual eminence of the "Angry Liberal" or the widespread seething of twenty-first-century Liberals. In those days, it was the Liberals who boasted of their sunny view of mankind, while claiming that the conservatives were the sourpusses. Liberals believed fervently in the possibility of mankind's improvement, even in mankind's perfection. At the time, one of the Liberals' complaints against the conservatives was that their view of mankind was "pessimistic," for conservatives were perpetually skeptical of the Liberals' perfection projects and even their mere improvement projects. Actually, the Liberals were as wrong about the conservatives' view of mankind as Schlesinger's definition of conservatism was wrong. The conservatives' view of mankind was neither pessimistic nor optimistic but rather that of the Founding Fathers, who envisaged mankind's nature as divided, capable of both good and evil depending on one's use of free will.

As for the Liberals' inhospitable encounter with the New Conservatism, perhaps we should sympathize with their early sourness. As in the twenty-first century, the Liberals of the early post–World War II period were not accustomed to disagreement, and these intellectual newcomers disagreed with them on almost everything. The traditionalists laughed at the Liberal improvement projects. The anti-Communists and the advocates of limited government were equally hostile to the Liberals. Given the Liberals' smugness, this wide-ranging set of rebukes must have been deeply disturbing. But the New Dealers had disturbed their era's status quo, many of whose stand-paters were still alive and now apparently striking back.

It is worth noting the New Deal's huge disruption of what had been laissez-faire America. President Roosevelt extended the federal government into areas previously off-limits to American government. During the New Deal, the federal government grew from gnawing on about 1 percent of GDP to consuming 11.18 percent. Then the exigencies of World War II necessitated an even larger percentage of GDP for the government's digestive tract (in 1945 the figure hit 47.9 percent and was still at 15.25 percent in 1950). This was a staggering growth, unparalleled until the Obama presidency.

Henry Regnery, one of the earliest protagonists of the New Conservatism, whose publishing house, Henry Regnery Company, published many of the movement's greatest thinkers (for instance, F. A. Hayek, Ludwig von Mises, Milton Friedman, Russell Kirk, and Buckley), offered a vivid glimpse as to how a New Conservative viewed the change imposed on Main Street by the New Deal. He told his son, Al, that while growing up in the Chicago area in the 1920s, the only manifestation he ever saw of the federal government was the massive post office in the center of suburban Hinsdale, its interior adorned with tall columns, its walls covered in marble, eagles atop the columns. By the late 1930s manifestations of the federal government were everywhere: the Blue Eagle of the National Recovery Administration, the projects of the Public Works Administration and of the Works Project Administration. Regnery and people who thought like him were, by the late 1940s, ready to put limits on government and challenge Liberals across a whole range of issues.

The hostilities between the Liberals and the New Conservatives were intense from the start. They endured and steadily intensified in large part because of a peculiar disagreement over Communism, specifically over Communist domestic espionage during the New Deal. As the Cold War passed from decade to decade, conservatives increasingly charged many of the Liberals with being at first "soft on Communism." Eventually they charged Liberals with being inept at foreign policy, given to starry-eyed abstractions and timorousness. Such charges would have been harmless in the 1940s; by the 1960s they worked.

In the early post–World War II period, many Liberals were themselves staunchly anti-Communist, and President Harry Truman was tough-minded on foreign policy—so much so that a later generation of Liberals blamed him for antagonizing Stalin and instigating the Cold War. Anti-Communist Liberals in the late 1940s distanced themselves from Communist sympathizers or Liberals they deemed insufficiently anti-Communist by setting up the Americans for Democratic Action (ADA). They claimed their anti-Communist brand of Liberalism was at the "vital center" of American political life. The term was coined by

Schlesinger. He and such intellectuals as John Kenneth Galbraith, and Reinhold Niebuhr, along with labor leaders such as Walter Reuther of the United Auto Workers (UAW), created the ADA to rid Liberalism of the likes of former vice president Henry Wallace, whose campaign for the presidency in 1948 was surrounded by fellow travelers and Communists.

Even as the ADA was forming, however, a controversy over the extent of Communist espionage in recent Democratic administrations created friction among anti-Communist Liberals that over time persuaded many to ally with the New Conservatives. These anti-Communists remained with the conservative movement until the end of the Cold War, providing conservatism with one of its strongest constituencies and most resonant issues. So essential was anti-Communism to the conservative movement that with Communism's collapse and the Cold War's conclusion in the early 1990s, conservatism's obituaries were again being composed.

Ironically, many of the anti-Communists of the conservative movement might never have joined the New Conservatism were it not for the demands of domestic partisan politics. When in the late 1940s Democrats were faltering in the polls, they made what was to be a fateful political decision. They closed ranks against Republican demands that they investigate domestic espionage during the administrations of Roosevelt and now Truman. As Republicans named suspected spies, the Democrats came to their defense. In so doing they allowed such Republicans as Congressman Richard Nixon and Senator Joseph McCarthy to become national figures. They also set in motion a contest between Liberals and conservatives that eventually (1) strengthened conservatives' claims of being more trustworthy in foreign policy and (2) alienated Liberals from ordinary Americans.

The process began with Liberals proclaiming the innocence of such New Dealers as Alger Hiss, a defense that lasted for years. Soon the Liberals were accusing ordinary Americans of participating in a "Red Scare." As the controversy lengthened and passions heightened, the dominant Liberal opinion became anti-anti-Communist, with some Liberals going so far as to blame Truman and his secretary of state Dean Acheson for causing the Cold War. By the late 1960s many of these Liberals opposed the use of force in foreign policy, becoming active members of the "peace movement" and nuclear disarmament. By the Reagan administration, they were accusing proponents of a strong foreign policy of being a greater danger to world peace than the Soviets, and President Reagan of wanting to "blow up the world."

Mileposts along the way in this Liberal radicalization were the Liberals' abandonment of their own Great Society president, Lyndon Johnson, during the Vietnam War. Another was President Jimmy Carter remonstrating against America's "inordinate fear of Communism."[6] Finally, there was the clarifying moment at the 1984 Republican Convention when Jeane Kirkpatrick, herself an ex-Liberal, inveighed against the Liberal Democrats as the "blame America first crowd."[7]

Today we have reason to know that the issue of domestic espionage that set off this chain of events never should have become such a vexed issue or one that lasted so long. In some places, for instance at the left-wing *Nation* magazine, it is still going on. As mentioned earlier, the controversy strengthened conservatism and alienated Liberals from the recent American past and from mainstream Americans. Through it all, our intelligence community was sitting on irrefutable evidence that the accused spies were, for the most part, spies.

From the beginning of the controversy in the late 1940s, Liberals have filled *Kultursmog* with doubts about spies in government and about anti-Communists in general. Given Liberals' proud regard for human rights, their reluctance to remain staunchly anti-Communist demonstrates yet again the potential for partisanship to overwhelm principle. Communism sounded the death knell to human rights wherever it prevailed, and the carnage it left is staggering. In 1997 *The Black Book of Communism: Crimes, Terror, and Repression*, compiled by European Social Democrats, placed the death toll at between 85 and 100 million people. Yet by the time of its publication, so tortured had the Liberals' argument with their anti-Communist rivals become that many were citing the collapse of the Soviet Union as proof that the Cold War was a waste of resources that put the United States on a path to reckless foreign policy. Soviet Communism, their argument ran, would have collapsed

"inevitably" as a consequence of its economic failure.*
Here is but another example of partisanship overwhelming
reason.

Actually, it was the ongoing partisan quarreling over
Communism—not the Cold War—that was the waste of
resources. The years of acrimony, however, and the con-
torted positions Liberals took in continuing the quarreling
illustrate one of my most fondly held beliefs about politics,
to wit, rather than appealing to ideas or even to material
interests, politics frequently appeals to psychological needs,
often the need to have enemies or at least some lunkhead to
feel superior to. Nineteenth-century British historian
Thomas Babington Macaulay deposited a similar finding in
his essay "The Earl of Chatham": "It is the nature of parties to retain their original enmities far more firmly than
their original principles."[8]

---

*This fashionable judgment is amusingly at odds with the 1984
observations of one of the Liberals' most esteemed economists,
John Kenneth Galbraith, who just before the Soviet collapse saw no
problems with Communism's command economy. In a September
3, 1984, New Yorker piece, he wrote "that the Soviet economy has
made great material progress in recent years is evident both from
the statistics . . . and from the general urban scene . . . One sees it
in the appearance of solid well-being of the people on the streets,
the close-to-murderous traffic, the incredible exfoliation of apart-
ment houses, and the general aspect of restaurants, theaters, and
shops . . . Partly, the Russian system succeeds because, in contrast
with the Western industrial economies, it makes full use of its manpower." Also the equally distinguished Liberal economist Lester
Thurow was referring to the Soviet economy's "remarkable performance." (Lester C. Thurow and Robert L. Heilbroner, The Economic
Problem, 7th ed. [Englewood Cliffs, NJ: Prentice Hall, 1984], 629.)

Liberals high in government, such as Dean Acheson, knew perfectly well that there were Communists of some sort in the Roosevelt administration. They thought little of it, and perhaps understandably. Russian Communists had effectively propagandized an emollient message. They were saving the world's working class. Before Stalin's abrogation of the Yalta Accords and the Soviet enslavement of Eastern Europe, the Communists trundling down the halls of the State Department and the U.S. Treasury could be viewed by their fellow New Dealers as humanitarians, or as the phrase had it, "progressives in a hurry."[9] At worst they were frivolous eccentrics, not much different from any of the other oddballs in their government—and there were plenty of oddballs in the New Deal. Consider Dr. Maurice Parmelee and how peacefully the New Dealers disposed of him.

Dr. Parmelee worked at the Board of Economic Warfare in the early 1940s under Vice President Henry Wallace. Dr. Parmelee was a learned fellow, a member of the American Association for the Advancement of Science and of the American Anthropological Society. He also was a conspicuous advocate of "universal nudism" at work and at play, until, at the behest of Congress, Wallace's top aide, Milo Perkins, fired him. That he was ever hired tells us a lot about the New Deal's openness to nonconformity.

Dr. Parmelee had been the butt of ridicule in the 1920s by such popular literary figures as George Jean Nathan. Even to cosmopolitans he was a joke. Nathan mocked him for writing such silliness as, "Nudity aids materially in bringing mankind closer to nature and in promoting more genuine and sincere relations between the sexes."[10] His risible notoriety notwithstanding, Dr. Parmelee was brought aboard by the New Dealers, who placed him in one of their great bureaucracies. Yet, when he was let go, there was none of the hullabaloo associated with Hiss's government service, just some good-natured joshing by the president, after which the scandal blew over. After Congressman Martin Dies turned the heat up on the nudist at the Board of Economic Warfare, FDR let the naked bureaucrat go. Then the president gave the country a lesson in crisis management. At a White House press conference he admitted that Parmelee was indeed a nudist, but Dies—a Democrat—was worse. He was, joked FDR, "an exhibitionist."[11] Had the Democrats dealt as deftly with Communists in government as they handled nudists, McCarthyism and all the attendant controversies following it might have amounted to but a footnote in history.

The New Deal employed many fine minds, but it also employed many exotics along with the aforementioned naked bureaucrat and Alger Hiss. Over at the Treasury Department, there was Harry Dexter White and Lauchlin Currie, who went on to become an economic adviser to the President. The Communist sympathies of Hiss, White, Currie, and others were widely suspected. I actually knew a former Treasury Department official, Huntington Cairns, later secretary of the National Gallery of Art, who in retirement in the late 1970s told me he had no doubt that White, in his Treasury days, was a Communist. Huntington was neither on the left nor the right but basically nonpolitical. He had no ax to grind. It was only when Communism's threat to the Western way of life became a national issue in the late 1940s that Communists in government became a serious controversy. The New Dealers should simply have fired their Communists, allowed justice to be done in the cases of treason, and been done with the problem.

Unfortunately, in the late 1940s, with the Democrats losing power and the Republicans exploiting the Communist issue, Democrats felt they needed to close ranks to stay in power, much as they were to close ranks fifty years later when President Clinton's lies under oath were revealed and his impeachment seemed likely. Acheson defended his friend Hiss publicly, despite the fact that Secretary of State James Byrnes had told Acheson as early as 1946 that the FBI and other sources were convinced that Hiss was a spy. Acheson actually advised Hiss to accept an offer at the Carnegie Endowment rather than face looming charges within the government of his Communist activities.[12]

For five decades the evidence against Hiss has steadily accumulated in one of the longest controversies in American history. In the 1990s the evidence reached critical mass. Following the fall of the Soviet Union, historians working within the Soviet archives found documents identifying Hiss as an agent. Since then this evidence has been cross-referenced with documents released in 1995 from the Venona project, making the case against Hiss irrefutable. The Venona project began in 1943 when the U.S. Army's Signal Intelligence Service (predecessor to today's National Security Agency) began intercepting and decrypting messages between Moscow and its agents in the United States.

The Army's interest was to discover whether Stalin was planning a negotiated peace with Hitler. It gave the project so high a security rating that even President Harry Truman was kept out of the loop. In 1950 Venona decoders decrypted a Soviet message sent from Washington to Moscow five years earlier. Its contents identified Hiss as an agent of Soviet military intelligence (GRU). Apparently, he had been working for the Soviets for a decade.

For the next half century, intelligence officers who had worked on the Venona project watched Liberals and conservatives quarrel with one another over whether there were Communists in the New Deal and who they might be. Yet these intelligence officers remained silent. Even today the theme of an unwarranted "Red Scare" is taught in high schools and universities. The Venona sleuths could have ended the controversy by making public their decrypts, which showed that for the most part the anti-Communists were right. Venona had discovered that as many as 349 Americans had been communicating with Soviet agents, including Currie, Hiss, and White.[13] Instead, until his death in 1996, Hiss was free to portray himself as a victim of anti-Communist hysteria. In doing so he duped those Liberals who imagined him to be a typical intellectual beset by conservative anti-intellectuals. His dramatization of himself as a victim of anti-Communist paranoia encouraged the Liberals in their devolution from anti-Communism to anti-anti-Communism, creating Jeane Kirkpatrick's "blame America first gang."

Perhaps in the aftermath of the Venona decrypts' revelations it is too early to ask why the Venona officials remained silent about their knowledge of Communist spies in government. Possibly they thought that going public would be a breach of an intelligence officer's nondisclosure agreement. Yet surely intelligence officers at the top of the intelligence community could have gone to the president or someone else high up in the national security apparatus. Some argue that the Venona sleuths kept quiet out of fear that by going public they would reveal to the world that they had cracked the Soviets' codes. Yet, this does not make much sense either. Our agents knew that the Soviets had become aware of Venona in 1948. How did our agents find out? They discovered that an American working in the Venona project was spying for the Soviets. His name was William Weisband Sr. Now, did Liberals high in government order the intelligence officers to remain silent lest their anti-Communist rivals be vindicated? Or was the silence another example of an intelligence bureaucracy's hidebound inaction?

Either way, had the Venona decrypts been made public in 1950 rather than in 1995, Liberals would have had one less complaint against America. They and their conservative adversaries would have one less complaint against each other. Only in the early twenty-first century are historians taking the existence of the Venona decrypts into account and noting, as British historian David Reynolds has in his new history of the United States, that "the new Red Scare [of the post–World War II period] had a foundation in fact."[14] Yet in the *Kultursmog* the facts remain hazy. The history texts used on college campuses mention Hiss and the espionage controversies of the post–World War II era, but none confirms that he was guilty.

By the end of the 1950s, the three constituent elements of the modern conservative movement were well established. Perhaps at that point a pithy definition of modern American conservatism could have been arrived at, but conservatism was still growing and attracting other groups whose members were becoming disaffected from Liberalism. Like Burke's organic society, conservatism was growing. By the late 1960s and early 1970s, certain Liberals and leftists, for instance former Trotskyites, were becoming restive over Liberalism's weakening will to govern. Here was the nucleus of what soon would be called neoconservatism. Its members were alarmed when Liberalism did not toughen its stand against Russian and Chinese Communism. They sensed that Liberal spinelessness was rendering ungovernable universities and cities, two longtime Liberal strongholds. In fact, the neoconservatives diagnosed all of American education as being in decline. A final source of their alarm was the rise of violence both in the general public and among various kinds of protestors, for instance, protestors within the civil rights movement, the peace movement, and left-wing student groups. These disaffected Democrats were mostly intellectuals, occasionally labor union activists. Such names as Irving Kristol and Jeane Kirkpatrick were featured on their marquees. Most became supporters of "the Reagan Revolution."

Also entering the conservative movement at about this

time were working-class ethnics who were soon to be known as "Reagan Democrats." Finally, as the Liberal penchant for disturbing the peace began to disturb settled American practices such as prayer in public places and restrictions against pornography and abortion, people of faith, often evangelicals but also Catholics, joined the conservative movement. All these migrants to the right made American conservatism by the 1980s something more than the New Conservatism of the 1950s and more difficult to define.

Liberalism has not experienced the growth that conservatism has and can boast of none of conservatism's diversity, though diversity is one of Liberalism's most harped-on values. What diversity Liberalism has experienced is merely the identity politics of those liberal-leaning malcontents who have cultivated through the years ever more grievances, for instance, feminists, homosexual activists, adepts of racial or ethnic politics, and of course the consumerists and environmentalists. The last two in particular are simply leftists who have adopted "consumerism" or "environmentalism" to mask their opposition to commerce and to private developers. Reminiscent of guests at a masked ball, they are given to intrigue. Since the 1960s they have practiced what I have called Masked Politics, opposing the Giant Corporations, land developers, and new technologies that give them endless anxieties and visits to their gastroenterologists. Behind the benign mask of a cautious consumerist or a pious environmentalist, most are simply old-fashioned socialists, though very few commentators have perceived the sham.

Liberals—masked or otherwise—have tended to divide Americans by exploiting the gripes of malcontents and pessimists. Meanwhile, conservatives have embraced an ever wider array of Americans, welcoming them to our shared values irrespective of their gripes. These clearly observable facts notwithstanding, throughout the *Kultursmog* the charge circulates that conservatives practice divisive politics. Allegedly the conservatives divide the citizenry by race or gender, though no racial or sexist slogans or invidious policies are ever adduced as evidence. This comes as no surprise. No member of the conservative movement has ever been a public bigot. On the right, George Wallace and the early Strom Thurmond were bigots, but Wallace was never part of the conservative movement, and Thurmond's open bigotry faded by the 1980s. On the Democratic side of the aisle, there were Liberals who were bigots, such as Arkansas's Senator J. William Fulbright and West Virginia's Senator Robert Byrd, who served in the Senate into the twenty-first century. Like Fulbright and Thurmond, Byrd's bigotry evanesced during middle age, but unlike them, he began his political career as an actual Klansman, a recruiter who, as a certified "Kleagle" in the early 1940s, corralled 150 galoots to start a Klan chapter in his hometown, Crab Orchard, West Virginia. The future Democratic leader charged each Klansman a ten-dollar membership fee and three dollars for an official robe and hood.[15] There actually were even Liberal Democrats in the last half of the twentieth century who rose from racist roots. Jimmy Carter played the race card early in his career. Yet no member of the conservative movement ever on the national stage was a race baiter.[16] The only simulacra of evidence that the Liberals can advance of conservatives' bigotry is that conservatives frequently disagree with the ideological policies of civil rights groups or of feminists. Policy disagreement, however, is not bigotry.

I use the term "ideological policies" advisedly. A fundamental point of disagreement that conservatives have with Liberals is that Liberals are ideologues. Conservatives usually are not. On the outer fringes of libertarianism, there are libertarian ideologues, but most conservatives are governed, as we shall see when we arrive at our definition of conservatism, not by ideology but by temperament. An ideologue is an adherent to a set of ideas and policies by which he judges a society and toward which he wants to direct society—whether society's members want to be directed or not. The ideologue is a social engineer. In his capacity as social engineer, the Liberal will tell you where to live, which bus will take your children to which school, how many members of a race or gender are to be in your group, your employment force, or your classroom. By contrast, the conservative stands for liberty, the Bill of Rights, and the mild tug of traditions, traditions that will always be changing but that usually comfort us as we gambol and stumble through life. The conservative perfectly understands the title Grover Norquist adopted for his book on modern conservatism, *Leave Us Alone*, wherein he says conservatives belong to the Leave Us Alone Coalition—well put.

Ever since the Reagan presidency, the smokestacks of the *Kultursmog* have pumped out the myth that conservatives intent on cutting taxes, deregulating industry, privatizing government services, or strengthening the military are acting as ideologues. In the *Kultursmog* it is understood that ideologues are unreasonable enthusiasts, often given to unworkable political projects dangerous to the commonweal—the kind of projects Burke warned about while witnessing the French Revolution. When Liberals use the term, it is a term of disparagement, which they disdainfully apply to conservatives. Yet when they are calling conservatives ideologues, they are again engaged in Masked Politics. Behind their masks of sweet reason, it is they who are the ideologues. Conservatism is not an ideology but, as the great conservative political philosopher Michael Oakeshott has explained, a "disposition."[17] The fact that conservatism is but a disposition explains why the conservative's political libido is restrained while the Liberal's is famously inclement.

Ideology is a word that has undergone many changes since the Frenchman Destutt de Tracy introduced it in the late eighteenth century as meaning the "science of ideas." Shortly thereafter, in the early nineteenth century Napoleon conferred on the word the deprecatory sense that makes Liberals don their masks and apply it to conservatives. Napoleon applied the word to the zealots of the French Revolution, whose enthusiasms for abstraction and for balmy projects were the ruin of France and a threat to his well-run army. Had he not thwarted them, he never would have become an emperor, and his army might never have gotten to a battlefield on time. The French Revolutionaries even imposed their abstractions on time.

They dreamed up a revolutionary calendar, revising months, days, and even the clock. It led to all sorts of impractical results that brought France ever more grief. Unsurprisingly, no other country adopted the Revolutionary clock. Not even President Barack Obama has shown an interest in it. If Napoleon were forced to use it, he might have found himself ordering his troops into battle about the time that, according to the Revolutionary clock, his infantry was expecting lunch or his cavalry's horses all had to go to the bathroom. The revolutionaries' exaltation of reason that struck Burke as cruel and tyrannical struck Napoleon as imbecilic. Ever since Napoleon's denunciations, the ideologue has been suspected of imposing impractical academic schemes on ordinary life, which is precisely what Liberals often do. The Liberal imposes such ideological constructs as diversity, income redistribution, and gender or racial quotas on society, while deviously denying their ideological designs. The conservative implements tax cuts that actually spur economic growth, and is dismissed by the Liberal as an ideologue. Tax cuts, of course, are popular with ordinary Americans. Quotas and income redistribution are not. The Liberals' recourse is to the *Kultursmog*, where they just pump out more *smog*: "Tax cuts are unpopular and cause deficits!" "Quotas and income redistribution are a matter of justice, and people love them!" "Only bigots oppose them!" Here again, the Liberal is engaged in Masked Politics.

Michael Oakeshott set down his finding that conservatism is a disposition in an essay still popular with many conservative intellectuals, "On Being Conservative." There the distinguished British philosopher explains that, rather than being an ideology, conservatism is a disposition, one that favors, he says, "the present." As he analyzes conservatism, conservatives—unlike Liberals—rarely seek to impose ideas or policies on the present unless the present is "arid" or "remarkably unsettled." Those ideas or policies that conservatives actually impose on society will not be the academic contrivances of revolutionaries or of hell-bent reformers, but what Oakeshott would perceive as being tried and true. Where conservatism is au fond a disposition toward the present, Liberalism is au fond an anxiety about the present. Keeping this analysis in mind, we can understand the origin of Liberalism's one unwavering political value laid bare in chapter 1, namely: to disturb the peace. Once we understand that it is personal anxiety that provokes the Liberals' petty crimes against society, the bloom is off their claims to noble visions and humanitarian reforms. Armed with an awareness of Liberalism's anxious nature, conservatives will be better prepared for the Liberals' furious opposition. A disposition is always more nonchalant than an anxiety.

Appearing in 1956, "On Being Conservative" suggests the differences between an ideology and a disposition when Oakeshott writes that conservatism is "not a creed or a doctrine, but a disposition.[18] The disposition "is to prefer the familiar to the unknown, to prefer the tried to the untried, fact to mystery, the actual to the possible, the limited to the unbounded, the near to the distant, the sufficient to the superabundant, the convenient to the perfect, present laughter to utopian bliss."[19]Thus we are more at ease with the world than our Liberal friends, driven as they are by what psychiatrists identify as "free-floating anxiety." After our first martini there is laughter; after the Liberal's somebody could get hurt, or at least suffer an embarrassing incident.

Oakeshott, presumably with Schlesinger's 1955 burlesque of the New Conservatism in mind, elaborated on the characteristics of the conservative disposition:

> They centre upon a propensity to use and to enjoy what is available rather than to wish for or to look for something else; to delight in what is present rather than what was or what may be. Reflection may bring to light an appropriate gratefulness for what is available, and consequently the acknowledgement of a gift or an inheritance from the past; but there is no mere idolizing of what is past and gone [a shot at Schlesinger?]. What is esteemed is the present; and it is esteemed not on account of its connections with a remote antiquity, nor because it is recognized to be more admirable than any possible alternative [another shot?], but on account of its familiarity.[20]

To be sure, there are restless, impulsive conservatives. Newt Gingrich comes to mind. However, the true conservative will put golf before the meetings of "concerned citizens," the cocktail hour before a flag burning, and a day at the office before flying off to the Indus Valley to sit at the feet of a swami or to Scandinavia to arrange a sex change.

Oakeshott also explains how conservatives are roused to political action, albeit reluctantly:

> If the present is arid, offering little or nothing to be used or enjoyed, then this inclination [this disposition to use or enjoy] will be weak or absent; if the present is remarkably unsettled, it will display itself in a search for a firmer foothold and consequently in a recourse to and an exploration of the past; but it asserts itself characteristically when there is much to be enjoyed, and it will be strongest when this is combined with evident risk or loss. In short, it is a disposition appropriate to a man who is acutely aware of having something to lose which he has learned to care for; a man in some degree rich in opportunities for enjoyment, but not so rich that he can afford to be indifferent to loss.[21]

That "something to lose," for modern conservatives, has been individual liberty, and it has been infringements on individual liberty that have incited conservative activism from the days of the New Deal to the present collectivism of Obamaism. The New Conservatism was roused by the New Deal. The Reagan Revolution was roused by the Great Society. The Republicans' Contract with America was roused by premonitions in the early Clinton administration of a return to big government, particularly in the area of health care. Always conservatism's impetus has been to preserve individual liberty, as warranted by the Constitution and the Declaration of Independence.

In the 1950s and 1960s, Frank Meyer, a senior editor to the New Conservatism's leading magazine, *National Review*, became the intellectual strategist and practitioner of Oakeshott's lyrical philosophizing. Through his national lecture tours, his service as the magazine's book review editor, and his political column in the magazine, aptly titled "Principles and Heresies," he refined the movement's principles and resolved disagreements among the movement's first constituent groups—the anti-Communists, the traditionalists, and the libertarians. In the case of the last two groups, he developed a political analysis that kept them together when they were perhaps at the point of breaking away from each other and slipping into obscurity. The analysis was dubbed "fusionism," by his friend L. Brent Bozell, Bill Buckley's brother-in-law. Frank did not like the term, but he accepted it, and it caught on.

A graduate of Oxford's Balliol College, Frank was an active Communist through the 1930s. Working in Chicago, he became one of the Party's most effective organizers, and after he broke with the Party in the 1940s an effective anti-Communist. He left the Communist Party with at least two invaluable troves of knowledge, the nature and practice of Marxist-Leninist ideology and the locations of all the best restaurants in Chicago. The Reds' appreciation of history might have been defective, but not their appreciation of cuisine. Frank raised the epicurean standards of the conservative movement as well as its standards of political analysis.

From his modest house on a quiet rural road up a mountain in Woodstock, New York—for a while Bob Dylan lived down from it—Frank read and wrote and telephoned fellow members of the New Conservatism all over the country from dusk to dawn. Fearing that the Communists would kill him in his sleep, he slept by day and worked from wake-up time, around 4:00 p.m., until bedtime, around 8:00 a.m. He slept with a shotgun at his bedroom door. Chain-smoking through the night and alternating coffee with an occasional tumbler of Scotch, he cultivated a network of anti-Communist, traditionalist, and libertarian intellectuals to review books for *National Review* and organize throughout the country. In the early 1960s, when a serious break between traditionalists and libertarians threatened the unity of the movement, he kept them together with fusionism, which mined the best thought of both groups and demonstrated their coherence.

As a member of the conservative movement's two youth groups, the Intercollegiate Studies Institute (originally founded as the Intercollegiate Society of Individualists in 1952, when Buckley and other founders of the modern conservative movement were more comfortable calling themselves individualists than conservatives) and the Young Americans for Freedom, I spent as much time with him as I could. He was a born prof, who relished speaking on campus and developing the next generation of conservative intellectuals and activists. I, as editor in chief of a conservative student magazine, had little difficulty becoming one of his friends before his untimely death at age sixty-two from lung cancer. In terms of intellect and selfless energy, there has been no one to equal him since.

Usually I visited with him when he was on one of his frequent speaking tours. I only spent one working night with him in Woodstock, but it was a memorable one. From New York City I brought along a young friend whom I knew Frank would see as a potential conservative activist, Bill Kristol, the son of the emerging "Godfather" of neoconservatism, Irving Kristol. I was a graduate student, working on a PhD in American history. Bill was a high school student. Even then Bill was not what you would call a neoconservative. At a very early age, Bill was pretty much a movement conservative, exuberantly to the right of his father. We arrived around dusk; had dinner at Frank's usual time, 8:30 p.m.; and for the rest of the night talked about politics, philosophy, the arts, and sports. Bill was too young to drink. I compensated. Until we all turned in after breakfast at 6:00 a.m., it was a raucous night punctuated by Frank's long-distance calls to his apparatchiks and book reviewers and by cups of coffee alternately taken with the Scotch. Frank had a theory: coffee kept him alert; Scotch kept him relaxed.

After our brief retreat to sleep, we were awakened by his graceful wife, Elsie, who led us to my car and the bleary drive back to Manhattan. Mark that night down as one of the most grueling nights I have ever spent. Dancing at a Manhattan nightclub until dawn can be hard on the liver and other interior plumbing, but trying to keep up with Frank was far more punishing. By the time we got back to the Kristol family's Manhattan flat to greet Irving and his wife, the historian Gertrude Himmelfarb, I suspect we looked more like we had spent the previous twenty-four hours with Frank's neighbor, Bob Dylan, than with the book review editor of *National Review*.

Having rejected Communism and found refuge in the writings of the Founding Fathers, Frank propounded "freedom of the person" as fundamental to American conservatism.[22] Using the words *freedom* and *liberty* interchangeably in his writing, he considered freedom "the central and primary end of political society."[23] To him "the person" was a thinking and autonomous creature; "freedom was of the essence of his being."[24] Government must insure that freedom, but that freedom existed for the high purpose of allowing the individual to choose virtue. Yet virtue could not be imposed by the state, whether it was governed by Liberals or traditionalists. As Frank wrote, "Unless men are free to be vicious they cannot be virtuous. No community can make them virtuous."[25] He argued that government's end is to preserve freedom, and the citizen's end is to choose virtue. Always it is the individual who has to do the choosing.

Frank believed that libertarians and traditionalists were compatible in the conservative movement. Balancing freedom and virtue would be crucial for that alliance. He subscribed to the Founding Fathers' insight that freedom was the ultimate political end, but virtue was the ultimate end of man. Traditionalists and libertarians had different emphases. Traditionalists were soft on limited government. Libertarians were not in agreement on the importance or even the existence of virtue. Frank believed that the U.S. Constitution supplied the bridge between these two elements of conservative thought. Both had portions of what a serious political movement needed to protect the individual. Russell Kirk, author of *The Conservative Mind: From Burke to Santayana*, led the traditionalists in stressing order and virtue as apprehended through the Western experience by "right reason." Traditionalists would use the state to impose virtue, much as monarchies and nation-states had throughout much of Western history. F. A. Hayek, author of *The Road to Serfdom*, led the libertarians in stressing (A) individual liberty, (B) laissez-faire economics (now more popularly called free-market economics), and (C) reason. According to Frank, as long as the state was not used to impose virtue, and society developed democratically, the two elements of conservatism were compatible. He proved to be right.

Frank's position on government was strongly libertarian. Beyond national security, preservation of domestic order, and the administration of justice through the rule of law, state power should be limited. He feared, however, that the libertarian argument for freedom was shallow and needed to be fortified by accepting the traditionalists' insight that freedom was God-given, that virtue was important, and that many Western traditions strengthened the free society. The skepticism of some libertarians toward these three values weakened their defenses against statism, either secular statism or totalitarian statism.

As much a student of Western history as of Western philosophy, Frank believed that the God of Abraham endowed us with individual liberty. Unlike the classical liberals who admired liberty for its utility, he understood liberty as being more than merely useful. In creating man, God made freedom the "essence of his [man's] being." God did this so that his creatures could choose to be virtuous. We might also choose to be evil, but without God-given choice, virtuousness was impossible. Doubting that the libertarians' basis for freedom was as compelling against Communism and other statist regimes as was the traditionalists' divine basis for freedom, Frank opted for the traditionalists' basis. He came to believe in the traditionalists' God, converting to Catholicism on his deathbed.

His practical insight was that whatever one thought of virtue or of God, as long as neither was imposed on libertarians, they had no grounds to break with the conservative movement. From tradition and history, God and virtue would make their appearances in the American polity. As long as libertarians were comfortable in that polity, the conservative movement could endure and prosper. It has for nearly sixty years.

To hear David Frum and his Reformed Conservatives discourse on the adaptations conservatives must make to get elected, one might conclude that American conservatism is nothing more than a gimmick for attaining high office. Actually it is, as the founders of conservatism conceived it, an intellectual movement to preserve American values, pre-eminently the value of liberty. As an intellectual movement it will affect a wider realm than mere campaign politics. It will affect American society.

In the middle 1960s, as the conservative movement was gaining strength, Meyer laid out a series of "articles of belief" that most conservatives would accept to one degree or another today. They are worth repeating as a prelude to unveiling the definition of a political movement that has come from its three constituent elements (advocates of limited government, anti-Communists, and traditionalists) to embrace neoconservatives, evangelicals, Reagan Democrats, and many ordinary Americans made uneasy by the Liberals' feverish projects.

A. "Conservatism assumes the existence of an objective moral order based upon ontological foundations."

B. "Within the limits of an objective moral order, the primary reference of conservative political and social thought and action is the individual person."

C. "The cast of American conservative thought is profoundly anti-utopian."

D. "It is on the basis of these last two points— concern for the individual person and rejection of utopian design—that the contemporary American conservative attitude to the state arises . . . Conservatives may vary on the degree to which the power of the state should be limited, but they are agreed on the principle of limitation."

E. "Similarly, American conservatives are opposed to state control of the economy."

F. "American conservatism derives from these positions its firm support of the Constitution of the United States as originally conceived— to achieve the protection of individual liberty in an ordered society by limiting the power of government."

G. "In their devotion to Western civilization and their unashamed and unself-conscious American patriotism, conservatives see Communism as an armed and messianic threat to the very existence of Western Civilization and the United States.[26]

Presumably, today Frank would say that the same holds true for radical Islam, in all its configurations and guises.

To one degree or another, most of the members of today's conservative movement would accept these articles of belief. Even Americans who consider themselves conservative without giving any thought to being part of a movement would probably adhere to them, for as Oakeshott says, conservatism is a disposition, as he implies a reasonable disposition. Yet here let me take mild exception to Oakeshott's choice of the word disposition. Irving Kristol and Bill Buckley, too, accepted it, but a better word is temperament. Herb London, a formidable mind in contemporary conservatism, who heads the Hudson Institute, argues for the word, and I think he is right. A disposition could be dismissed as a mere mood. Temperament has more substance and consistency. It is a manner of acting, feeling, and thinking. In our time it is a better description of the origin of the conservative sensibility.

So now having moved from Richard Weaver to Oakeshott to Meyer, and having noted the constituencies that conservatism has picked up along the way, let me unveil a definition of modern American conservatism. It takes into account the Founding Fathers' love of liberty and Burke's fear of projects propelled by reason enthroned. It absorbs the neoconservatives' remonstrances against those projects' unintended consequences.

Conservatism is a temperament to delight in life, liberty, and the pursuit of happiness, including in that pursuit the desideratum that John Locke mentioned in his original variation of this theme, the acquisition and exchange of property. Modern conservatism is a temperament, not an ideology or an anxiety. It is a love of liberty, not a misdemeanor.

6

FOUNDED ON IDEAS

Principles and Policies as
Equipment for the Journey

Conservatism's recovery will be through an archipel-ago of public policy think tanks that did not exist during conservatism's earlier times of troubles. The intel-lectual reviews that have been established since the 1950s (for instance, the *National Review*, the *Weekly Standard*, and the *American Spectator*) will also help by spreading the ideas and policies of the think tanks to the magazines' well-established audiences. The whole process of recovery will be enhanced by the conservatives' New Media: talk radio, Fox News, and the Internet.

These think tanks were a major resource for the Reagan administration, for the Republican congressional ascendancy of the 1990s, and—to a lesser degree—for the administrations of both Bushes. There are a dozen or so of these institutions whose scope is national and international. There are also many smaller think tanks throughout the country whose scope is only statewide or limited to local issues, though they are useful resources in their locales.

Taken together, they are the accidental consequences of the Liberals' anti-intellectualism. One of the ironies of the *Kultursmog*'s isolation and misrepresentation of conservatives is that the Liberals have gotten the conservatism they deserve. At the top of the intellectual heap, they are confronted by tough-minded, learned, free-thinking intellects such as the American Enterprise Institute's (AEI) Charles Murray or the Hoover Institution's Thomas Sowell, both of whom are much more intellectually formidable than they might have been had they remained at the intellectually inhospitable and socially oppressive universities. At the more popular level, the Liberals are confronted by combative and occasionally crude conservative media personalities who gain much of their popularity from the Liberals' fussy indignation. Still, their influence cannot be ignored.

The conservatives' island chain of public policy think tanks traces back to F. A. Hayek's publication of *The Road to Serfdom* in London in 1944 and in America months later. Now acclaimed one of the most influential books of the twentieth century, its American edition introduced Hayek to a small audience of writers, academics, and businessmen who were growing impatient with the New Deal's collectivism and with the barbarism that they had recently beheld in Europe. The book introduced Hayek and his brand of classical liberalism—a philosophical position highly congenial to limited-government Americans—to a wider audience too. A condensed edition of it, produced by *Reader's Digest* in 1945, sold to more than 2 million of the magazine's subscribers. Naturally, the book did not get a very welcoming reception from academe or from conventional journalists on either side of the Atlantic. In fact, its frosty reception in America was very similar to the reception William F. Buckley Jr.'s *God and Man at Yale* was to receive a few years later. The book did, nevertheless, catch the eye of a British entrepreneur, Antony Fisher, who went on to become the Johnny Appleseed of the right-of-center think tank movement internationally. It also caught the attention of several remarkable American businessmen, in particular, William Volker, a German immigrant whose Kansas City dry goods fortune created the Volker Fund in the late 1940s; and Harry Earhart, whose Michigan petroleum supply fortune funded the Earhart Foundation. Both foundations helped fund Hayek's proposed intellectual war against socialism and statism. They were early funders of the scholars and think tanks that allied with Hayek in waging his war of ideas.

Fisher's money and energetic intelligence created the pioneering Institute for Economic Affairs (IEA) in London in 1955, the original free-market think tank whose monographs and books demolished socialism, advanced the free-market alternative, and after two decades made contact with a sympathetic politician, Margaret Thatcher. In the meantime Fisher brought the IEA prototype think tank to other English-speaking nations and to Latin America and Europe. Notable among his creations in the United States were the Atlas Economic Research Foundation, the Pacific Research Institute, and the National Center for Policy Analysis in Dallas. While he was doing this, the Earhart

Foundation in the late 1940s began supporting scholars whose work reshaped the economic world, among them the economists Gary Becker, James Buchanan, Ronald Coase, Milton Friedman, Hayek, and George Stigler—all eventually Nobel laureates. Earhart's largesse also went to nonacademics whose work contributed to the traditionalists in the rising conservative movement, for instance, philosophers Leo Strauss and Eric Voegelin, and eventually Allan Bloom, author of the 1987 best seller *The Closing of the American Mind*. The Volker Fund was equally important to nascent conservatism, and in 1947 it funded a contingent of thinkers' attendance at the first meeting of the Mont Pelerin Society, birthplace of the modern free-market movement. Though the Volker Fund and the Earhart Foundation did not actually found think tanks, they soon were contributing to them upon their establishment. Both AEI and the Hoover Institution received early grants. What is more, both foundations were early contributors to the development of young conservative intellectuals who would find their way into the think tanks and eventually into government service.

When *The Road to Serfdom* came out, none of this seemed possible. Hayek was a relatively unknown Austrian-born economist at the London School of Economics, propounding a classical liberal view of the world shaped by the writings of Adam Smith, David Hume, and Edmund Burke. Insisting that he was not a conservative but a liberal in the nineteenth-century sense, Hayek believed that any movement he might promote or be a part of would be called "liberal." He was right to see himself as a nineteenth-century liberal and to see most Americans critical of the New Deal as nineteenth-century liberals, too, but once the statist excesses of Nazism and Communism were observable for all to see, "liberal" used as a political term of identity sparkled and took on the attributes of an honorific, making it utterly impossible for Hayek to wrestle it from the clutches of opportunistic Americans on the left, who had also appropriated the honorific "progressive."

Their successful shanghaiing of the term *liberal* prompted Hayek to make an illuminating protest, which he filed in the preface to the 1956 edition of *The Road to Serfdom*. Much of the terminological confusion that Americans suffer to this day might have been avoided had Hayek had his way in maintaining *liberal* in its original sense. In 1956 he wrote:

> In current American usage it ["liberal"] often means very nearly the opposite . . . It has been part of the camouflage of leftish movements in this country, helped by the muddleheadedness of many who really believe in liberty, that "liberal" has come to mean the advocacy of almost every of kind of government control. I am still puzzled why those in the United States who truly believe in liberty should not only have allowed the left to appropriate this almost indispensable term but should even have assisted by beginning to use it themselves as a term of opprobrium.[1]

In truth, no one "allowed the left to appropriate this almost indispensable term." The Left stole it and embarked on one of its most momentous acts of Masked Politics. The Left's success in expropriating a term that rightly is synonymous with "limited government" has allowed President Obama to call himself a "liberal" while his administration undertakes to put ever more of the private sector under government control, denying ordinary Americans fundamental rights, for instance, the right to buy whatever health care they want, and the right for doctors to relate freely with their patients, unhindered by government regulations. Had Hayek won this battle, conservatives on the road to recovering our liberties would be called liberals, and Obama's collectivists would be called socialists. Finally, I would not have to resort to typographical contortions by distinguishing today's phony liberals with a capital *L*.

Hayek was more successful in demonstrating his book's two major points: (1) that socialism leads to tyranny and the diminishment of liberty and (2) that the remedy for socialism is classical liberalism as championed in America by proponents of limited government and as originally sketched out in the Constitution by the Founding Fathers. Hayek's proximate concerns were socialism, which was on the ascendancy in Europe—in London the Labour Party had taken control of the government and was taking over British industry—and in this country the New Deal's collectivists.

With *The Road to Serfdom*'s fame, Hayek became a galvanizing force for personal liberty and limited government. He took to the lecture circuit and also began to organize his kind of "liberals." His efforts were mostly on the intellectual front rather than in political activity, for he believed in, as James Piereson has written, "emphasis on the importance of ideas in the growth of political movements."[2] As a consequence, his early efforts were in the realm of ideas; and the early institutions that followed his influence, the first think tanks, were more scholarly than political. The more political think tanks came later.

Hayek's insistence on preserving eighteenth- and nineteenth-century ideas and applying them to contemporary political monstrosities would doubtless earn him the scorn of today's Reformed Conservatives and other 2008 critics of the conservative movement for being backward looking, possibly even "nostalgic." Yet Hayek's insights in the 1940s, based on the ideas of classical liberals, led years later to the political triumphs of Thatcher and Ronald Reagan. Likewise today the same centuries-old classical liberal ideas are animating intellectual work in the conservative think tanks where they are developing policies for the next generation of Thatchers and Reagans.

As an idea man, Hayek was greatly responsible for making the conservative movement an idea movement, though the Liberals were slow in recognizing that they were up against ideas rather than mere prejudices. Thinking, as he did, that ideas and principles were fundamental to a political movement, Hayek complained that bad ideas, mainly the bad ideas of Hegel and Marx, had seduced modern intellectuals, whom he called "secondhand dealers in ideas," and whose grasp of ideas he doubted.[3] Hayek's antidotes were the good Whig ideas from the eighteenth and nineteenth centuries, but they needed support, and while the good Whig ideas of the past received reliable support from enlightened aristocrats and owners of great country estates, in the 1940s Hayek for the most part had to rely on businessmen, whom he feared had a "tendency to orthodoxy."[4] One can understand his prejudice against modern businesspeople. Many have indeed sided with "orthodoxy," having been sedated by the *Kultursmog*. Consider even the brilliant prodigies of engineering and entrepreneurship who have prospered in Silicon Valley, men such as Microsoft's Bill Gates and Apple's Steve Jobs. The relatively free business climate of the Reagan years allowed them to thrive, improve American productivity, and fill our lives with technological marvels. Nonetheless, they have been slavish supporters of the very Liberals who now threaten commercial freedom and economic growth. In fact, most of the great fortunes of the country from Wall Street to Silicon Valley have funded Liberalism, as we shall see.

Perhaps to Hayek's surprise, independent businessmen like Fisher, Earhart, and Volker were there in what Piereson has identified as the first phase of conservative philanthropy. It began quietly with the Mont Pelerin Society. At the instigation of Hayek, the Society was founded in April 1947 at the Hotel du Pare in Switzerland, on the shores of Lake Geneva, where thirty-six classical liberals gathered in what was to become an annual meeting now held all over the world. William Volker's Volker Fund, provided a two-thousand-dollar grant to send a group of American free-market thinkers to the famous meeting at the Hotel du Pare, including the economists Milton Friedman, Frank Knight, Ludwig von Mises (another Austrian economist who had been Hayek's mentor and now lived in America), and George Stigler. The Volker Fund also sent three journalists whose writing ran against the grain of New Deal thought, John Davenport, Henry Hazlitt, and Felix Morley. Also sent at Volker's expense were two men who were building what today might be recognized as the prototypes of American conservative think tanks, Leonard Read of the Foundation for Economic Education, and F. A. Harper, soon to found the Institute for Humane Studies.

The Volker Fund went on to endow a chair for Hayek as a professor of moral science in the Committee on Social Thought at the University of Chicago. His title was lifted from Adam Smith's title at the University of Edinburgh, for Hayek's concerns were broader than simply economics. Volker also subsidized von Mises at New York University and the economist Aaron Director, Friedman's brother-in-law at the University of Chicago. In fact, the Volker Fund along with similar private donors gave significant assistance to what came to be called the "Chicago School" at the University of Chicago's department of economics and to professors and graduate students studying free-market economics elsewhere, for instance, at the department of economics at UCLA and at the University of Virginia's school of political economy under James Buchanan, another free-market winner of the Nobel prize.

Displaying "the paranoid style in American politics"

once diagnosed as a purely right-wing psychosis, but since Hillary Clinton's 1998 murmurings about a "vast right-wing conspiracy," now recognized as a psychosis suffered at both extremes of the political spectrum, the Left has always claimed that these free-market economists were the hired guns of the Giant Corporations or of enormously wealthy patrons. In the case of the Chicago School, the Left has even charged that one of its most illustrious economists served as the hired gun of fascists. In 1975 Friedman brought some University of Chicago economists—dubbed the "Chicago Boys"—to Chile to advise members of dictator Augusto Pinochet's government and some private citizens on how to revive Chile's economy, with the effect of making it to this day one of the healthiest in South America. Doubtless, Friedman would have helped the Red Chinese and the People's Republic of Bulgaria if either government had asked.

As for the Left's claim that the free-market economists of the New Right were the beneficiaries of the Giant Corporations or of Great Wealth, that, too, is a delusion produced by the paranoid style. Giant Corporations are easily intimidated and steer clear of controversy.

The fate of two other foundations important in helping to fund the first phase of conservative philanthropy is instructive, the Lilly Endowment and the Glenmede Trust, both being the creation of wealthy families with strong corporate pressures on them, the Lilly pharmaceutical family and the Pew family of Sun Oil. With the encouragement of the conservative Lilly family of Indianapolis and of J. Howard Pew, a conservative oil man from Philadelphia, these foundations supported the conservative movement in the 1950s and 1960s with grants similar to those given by the Volker Fund and the Earhart Foundation. After the deaths of the original Lilly patrons and of Pew, however, the foundations came under corporate pressure and in the Pew case, pressure from younger Pews to refrain from conservative philanthropy. Eventually Lilly became pretty much nonpolitical and Pew's Glenmede Trust was transformed into today's Pew Trusts, which is now a drearily reliable smokestack of the *Kultursmog*.

A long-standing challenge conservative philanthropy has faced has been how to keep conservative foundations independent of the *smog*. Not only has J. Howard Pew's philanthropy found itself taken over by Liberals, but another very conservative philanthropist, John D. MacArthur, lost his foundation, the John D. and Catherine T. MacArthur Foundation, to the *smog* upon his death.

In fact, it is a Liberal myth that the conservative movement has been funded by vast wealth. The claim is often made, but the truth is that the amount of money that went into the funding of the first phase of conservative scholarship, think tanks, and activism was a pittance compared to the funds then available to the Left. The funds spent by Volker, Earhart, Lilly, Glenmede, and other donors such as the Relm Foundation and the Liberty Fund amounted to an annual sum of around $3 million when the Ford Foundation alone was spending $300 million to fund the Left, in addition to the huge contributions made by the Rockefeller Foundation and the Rockefeller Brothers Fund.

By the second phase of conservative philanthropy, beginning in the mid-1970s, resources had increased; but still the conservative movement had nowhere near the available funds that the Left had. Augmented by support from the John M. Olin Foundation, the Smith Richardson Foundation, the Bradley Foundation, and foundations controlled by Richard M. Scaife, the conservatives' funding in 2003 amounted to perhaps $100 million annually with their five largest foundations controlling $1.5 billion in capital. By contrast, in the same year the five major Liberal foundations—Ford, Rockefeller, and MacArthur foundations, the Pew Trusts, and the Carnegie Corporation—had $24 billion in capital, with annual giving in the range of $1.2 billion.[5]

Though outspent hugely, the conservatives spent their money strategically, encouraging scholars and scholarly institutions in their first phase. Then in their second phase they extended their support to the whole range of thought embraced by the conservative movement, including religion, foreign policy, strategic issues, and the humanities.

According to Piereson, the man who defined the two phases of conservative philanthropy and is the most knowledgeable student of conservative philanthropy, "In contrast to Hayek and his followers, they [the foundations and think tanks of phase two] were also prepared to engage the world of politics and policy and to wage the war of ideas in a direct and aggressive style."[6] Thus the Heritage Foundation, a rapid-response think tank, the Federalist Society, and other lesser known organizations came into being. Also the conservative magazines became major players in the war of ideas. One of those magazines, *The New Criterion,* has confined its interest almost wholly to culture. In so doing, it has displayed how conservatism's conception of culture differs from that of Liberalism. Where the Liberal interest is in the neoteric, nihilistic, and often neurotic, the conservative conception of culture is aesthetic, humanistic, classical, and ennobling. As Oakeshott might explain, it is a vision born of a temperament rather than, as with Liberalism, an ideology.

Looking back on all this philanthropic activity and the think tanks and the magazines, Rick Cohen, former executive director of the National Committee for Responsive Philanthropy, offered an appraisal for the *New York Times*: "Unlike most liberal foundations, they've [the conservative foundations] put their money into organizations, rather than projects, to build the infrastructure of those very conservative organizations."[7] Cohen speaks of "infrastructure." I speak of an "archipelago." My guess is that he is a sociologist.

The contributions of Richard M. Scaife merit discussion here not only because they have been very generous and the embodiment of Cohen's assessment but also because Scaife himself is an example of the myths created by the Left's paranoia. A handsome patrician gentleman who in his middle seventies still has a full head of hair and a ready smile, Scaife was born to one of the great philanthropic families of America. He is the grand nephew of Calvin Coolidge's famed secretary of the treasury, Andrew Mellon, the founder of the National Gallery of Art. Scaife's mother, Sarah, was one of the principle heirs to the Mellon fortune and a woman whose philanthropies extended from the arts to population control and medicine. The Sarah Scaife Foundation funded Dr. Jonas Salk in his development of the polio vaccine.

Scaife's philanthropic endeavors date from the early 1960s when he became a supporter of Barry Goldwater. He donated a hefty sum to the 1968 campaign of Richard Nixon but was disappointed in Nixon. Having seen what the Liberals through their foundations were doing for think tanks such as the Brookings Institution and for organizations such as the American Civil Liberties Union, Scaife decided, as one of his aides put it, "to do the mirror image, but do it better."[8] A common complaint of today's Liberals is that the conservative movement's archipelago is somehow unique. As Scaife recognized, the Liberals' political philanthropy predated the conservatives. Their problem was— returning to Cohen's assessment—that they did not do it as well. Soon, with his superb team of aides, Scaife was doing it better than anyone.

That team, composed at first of Richard Larry and R. Daniel McMichael (both from US Steel), traveled the country, familiarizing themselves with the consequences of Hayek's early work, specifically, the scholars and the think tanks that by the 1960s were working across a broad range of social and political issues and applying classical liberal principles to modern problems. Scaifes's aides had an uncanny ability to "pick winners" without ever intruding into the winners' work. By phase two of conservative philanthropy, Scaife's foundations (he controlled three) were funding the established think tanks and heavily investing in the newer, more aggressive organizations, some of which they were crucial in establishing, for instance, the Heritage Foundation.

The work of Larry and McMichael puts one in mind of Machiavelli's intuition into the character of a leader. As the Florentine stated it in his famous classic *The Prince*, "The first opinion which one forms of a prince, and of his understanding, is by observing the men he has around him; and when they are capable and faithful, he may always be considered wise, because he has known how to recognize the capable and to keep them faithful."[9] Still, contrary to Liberal myth, Scaife has never limited his philanthropy to politics. Following in his family's philanthropic tradition, Scaife's foundations have generously contributed to the arts (for instance, the National Gallery of Art, the Brandywine Art Museum, the Westmoreland Museum of Art, and the Sarah Scaife Wing of the Carnegie Art Museum, which he built), conservation (for instance, the Phipps Conservatory), urban revival (for instance, Pittsburgh's Station Square Project) and the Pittsburgh History and Landmarks Foundation. Says an officer of this organization, Scaife "has been the quiet leader of urban revitalization in this city."

Scaife has a particularly avid interest in journalism, owning among other publications the *Pittsburgh Tribune-Review*, in which he is personally involved on a daily basis, and numerous regional publications. One particularly amusing story is his alleged involvement in the "Arkansas

Project," ritualistically referred to in the *Kultursmog* as a "secretive" investigative project run out of the *American Spectator* to "dig up dirt on Bill Clinton."[10] Actually Scaife's funding was merely for improving investigative reporting at the *Spectator* (designated clearly in his foundation's public disclosure reports as "Support for Expanded Editorial and Reporting") during the 1990s, when investigative reporting was all the rage. As it turned out, the Clinton administration's cavalcade of scandals comprised the dominant journalistic theme of the decade, and consequently most of the project's reportage dealt with the Clintons. Had the news been otherwise, Clinton stories would not have been as prominent.

The name itself, Arkansas Project, was a joke term in the office not because we started out being interested in the Clintons but because the Clintons' high jinks captured so much of our journalistic attention. A similar joke term probably could have been developed in the investigative unit of the *Washington Post*, if laughter were not *malum prohibitum* in that grisly newsroom. Surely the *Post*'s budget for covering the Clinton's antics was larger than the *Spectator*'s.

Scaife himself never was a "Clinton hater," to revive a term popular from the Clinton years, and rashly applied to almost any Clinton critic. His innocence of the charge is easily demonstrated by a couple of anecdotes, one quite amusing. Consistent with his philanthropic interest in historic preservation, Scaife has been a donor to the White House Endowment Fund, where his donations have been significant. When things got particularly heated for the Clintons following the Monica Lewinsky revelations, Scaife made one of his regular appearances at a White House reception for patrons of the White House Endowment Fund's restoration project. On the evening of January 21, 1998, shortly after the First Lady had apprised viewers of NBC's *Today Show* about the "vast right-wing conspiracy," whom did she and Bill meet in the receiving line but the charming silver-haired Scaife? Worse, they could not avoid having their picture taken with him by the White House photographer.

Scaife was amused, reporting that Bill was "red faced." The Clintons were *not* amused. Prompted by the *Washington Post* and CNN to obtain the picture, which according to custom, most White Houses routinely mail out, Scaife's lawyer, Yale Gutnick, had to enter into extended negotiations with the White House, braving several acrimonious calls from White House aide Sidney Blumenthal, who was suspicious as to Scaife's plans for the photograph— again the Left's paranoid style. All Scaife wanted was a copy for his desk, where it has rested since May 17, 1999, when it finally arrived in Pittsburgh—but without the letter from the president that Blumenthal had promised.

Nor was this the last time Scaife was to see Clinton. Impressed by the work of the Clinton Global Initiative, Scaife has met with the retired president in his New York office and donated generously to his humanitarian work in Africa. The inveterate philanthropist for conservative politics and for culture in general is also a humanitarian to the utmost and no hater of Clinton. Actually as he has said publicly he rather admires aspects of Clinton's work, particularly for poor Africans suffering from HIV. Depicted by Liberal myth to be "reclusive," Scaife is perfectly comfortable with the public and is at ease with a wide array of Americans, from the former president to the man on the street to the scholars at all the conservative think tanks that he endows.

There are now more than one hundred conservative think tanks across the country, but the big ones paving the way for conservatism's road to recovery are essentially seven. In them the ideas have been bubbling up. The policies have been laid out. Equally important, the personnel for future presidential administrations have been honing their skills and deepening their knowledge in each of their areas of expertise. For years, when Liberalism has been out of power, its personnel have returned to their universities, their jobs in the corporate world or the trade unions, and their chairs at various Liberal think tanks. Since the Nixon administration, conservatives have been doing much the same, but with most universities closed to them, they return in large numbers to their archipelago of think tanks whether as endowed fellows, visiting fellows, or merely attendees at seminars or participants in other programs. In Washington the American Enterprise Institute (AEI) contains so many former conservative members of the government that it is occasionally referred to as the home of the Republicans' "shadow government."

AEI is the oldest of the conservative movement think tanks. Founded in 1943, it was once merely a Republican research organization for public policy, but as the New Conservatism developed a self-conscious distinctness from the Tweedledum and Tweedledee nature of 1950s Republican and Democratic politics, AEI became more forthrightly conservative. It does have the distinction among conservative think tanks of being hospitable to moderate Democrats, particularly to those who in the 1960s and 1970s were called "Scoop" Jackson Democrats, whose eponym, Senator Henry "Scoop" Jackson, was the Cold War senator from the state of Washington.

The other major conservative movement think tanks are the Cato Institute; the Competitive Enterprise Institute (CEI); the Heritage Foundation; the Hoover Institution on War, Revolution and Peace; the Hudson Institute; and the Manhattan Institute for Policy Research. All of these organizations engage heavily in research on domestic and foreign policy, though with slightly different emphases.

The Manhattan Institute was one of Anthony Fisher's creations, founded by him in 1978 with the assistance of William J. Casey, soon to become President Reagan's director of central intelligence. Initially named the International Center for Economic Policy Studies, it was renamed in 1981. As one might expect, it has been heavily market oriented and particularly interested in urban problems. Mark that down as another example of the diversity of thought that characterizes conservatism, as opposed to Liberalism's serried ranks.

Of the major conservative think tanks, only the Manhattan Institute and the Hoover Institution are headquartered outside of Washington. Hoover, founded in 1959 at Stanford University by former President Herbert Hoover, originally had a unique interest in the U.S. Constitution, the Bill of Rights, and the rule of law as they militated against revolution and the kinds of despotism that had swept the twentieth century, particularly Communism. Consequently Hoover built up one of the greatest archives on revolution and Communism in the world, though now its faculty is more engaged with public policy and foreign policy, general politics and economics.

The Hudson Institute has offices both in Washington, D.C., and in New York City. It was founded by a kind of genius, futurist Herman Kahn, and focused on the kinds of questions a futurist might be expected to think about. With Kahn's death Hudson has, through the conventional think-tank practices of seminars, speakers programs, and in-house research, published—in monographs and books— findings on international security, freedom, and intelligence questions.

Another of the conservative think tanks that began from a unique perspective is the Cato Institute, which began very much as a strictly libertarian organization and has remained so to the point that its foreign policy position is markedly dovish compared with the foreign policy positions of the other conservative think tanks. There is a whiff of "Open Society" to Cato, but on such matters as the environment, the economy, and questions of personal liberty, it is what Liberals would call "right-wing," which is to say classical liberal or just liberal, properly understood.

As mentioned earlier, the Heritage Foundation is the

premier think tank founded during conservative philanthropy's second phase. It holds seminars and has a large
media presence, but its greatest distinction is that it
researches issues across a broad range for rapid response to
threats against free markets, individual liberty, and national
security. It also has a huge base of support, with more than
five hundred thousand individual, foundation, and corporate donors, and an annual budget today of more than $65
million.

Finally, there is the Competitive Enterprise Institute,
founded in 1984 to advance free market practices, oppose
government intervention, and keep America free of government meddling in the environment, technology, finance, and
public health. The Competitive Enterprise Institute makes
the unusual boast among conservative think tanks that it
takes its arguments to court when doing so is essential to
protect a competitive atmosphere for American commerce.

Bringing the war of ideas to the courts may be unusual
for conservatives, but Piereson has made an interesting discovery while writing about the philanthropy that went into
the creation of the conservative think tanks. Notwithstanding the Liberals' claims that the conservatives have, from
the Reagan era on, become exceptionally confrontational
and partisan, Piereson has discovered that Liberal philanthropy in the mid-1960s underwent a striking evolution
that may explain the fragmentation of Liberalism that
historian Sean Wilentz has written about or the "crack-up"
of Liberalism that I wrote about in my 1984 book, *The
Liberal Crack-Up*. Piereson's discovery may even shed light

on the emergence of the Angry Liberal who proved to be such a help for Democrats in 2008 and has been such a hindrance ever since, coaxing President Obama to the extreme left, threatening to abandon him if he softens, and in sum, repelling Independents.

At the Ford Foundation in 1966, its new president, McGeorge Bundy, once a Harvard dean and national security adviser to Presidents John F. Kennedy and Lyndon Johnson, introduced a kind of philanthropy called "advocacy philanthropy." It preferred activism to the usual research then done in Liberal think tanks to develop expertise in governance and public policy. "Soon," Piereson has written, "Ford and other liberal donors were investing in a maze of activist groups promoting feminism, affirmative action, environmentalism, disarmament, and other cutting-edge causes. The Environmental Defense Fund, the Natural Resources Defense Council, the Women's Law Fund, and the Mexican American Legal Defense and Education Fund, were among the products of this initiative."[11] All these groups advocated ideas, policies, legislation, and government regulations that could be manipulated in the courts and outside the normal electoral process on behalf of their ardent enthusiasms. The strategy funded by Bundy and others, says Piereson, "was well suited to philanthropic institutions with links to experts and advocates. And it led indisputably to results: employment quotas for women and minority groups, the expansion of welfare, new environmental legislation, and the like."[12] It also infiltrated narrowly focused fractious activists into the Democratic Party.

"Finally, liberalism itself came to be recast along interest-group lines," according to Piereson.[13] Surely this tumultuous metamorphosis sheds at least some light on the ancestry of 2008's Angry Liberal.

Neither of the Bushes resorted to the ideas and the personnel of the conservative movement as deliberately as did President Reagan or Newt Gingrich in his Republican congressional ascendancy. Curiously, President George H. W. Bush manifested some sort of reaction—was it personal or perhaps chemical?—to his predecessor, much as Prime Minister John Major reacted to Prime Minister Thatcher, and in both cases with electoral defeat as their reward. Both spurned the game book that had gotten them into office. President Bush's vow to create a "kinder, gentler nation" and his disavowal of his earlier "no new taxes" promise were genuflections to the *Kultursmog* that earned him no friends in the *smog* and defeat in 1992. As mentioned earlier, by the time of George W. Bush's presidency, the conservative movement was so dominant within the Republican Party that it could not be disavowed. In fact, President George W. Bush's court appointments and tax reductions were reflections of the work of the Federalist Society and of supply-side policies. Neither, however, represented the kind of deliberate choices that Reagan and Gingrich had made.

The explanation for George W.'s lack of conservative rigor was not a personal reaction against conservatism as much as the negligence of a man who, though more intelligent than his critics would grant him—his academic record actually surpassed those of his mediocre opponents, Vice

President Al Gore and Senator John Kerry—was not very interested in ideas. In the last months of Bush's presidency, Ed Gillespie, then a White House counselor and himself a movement conservative who had served as a top aide to another movement conservative, House majority leader Dick Armey, explained to me that before his 2007 arrival at the White House, hardly anyone on the staff was familiar with the conservative movement and its think tanks that by then were very much a part of the Washington scene.[14] To be sure, there were movement conservatives in the administration, for instance, Bush's first solicitor general, Ted Olson, a prominent member of the Federalist Society, or for that matter, Vice President Dick Cheney, a senior fellow in the 1990s at AEI who returned to AEI after his vice presidency.

But the Bush administration was famous for bringing in young, inexperienced supporters, often Texans, who were unaware of the intellectual political landscape. Unlike the Reagan administration, whose movement conservatives dutifully implemented the boss's conservative agenda, the Bush administration, though led by the first MBA to be president, had little reach into the federal bureaucracy. Some admittedly conservative policies were pursued: for instance, the reform of Social Security with "personal accounts" and of health care with Health Savings Accounts. The president's No Child Left Behind plan was supposed to have a robust school choice component, but it was sacrificed to win Democratic votes. A similar fate befell the private insurance component of his original Medicare prescription drug benefit plan. Ultimately, however, many policies developed in the conservative think tanks were left untried, and the froth of speechwriter Michael Gerson's philosophical contrivance, "Heroic Conservatism," suggests that some sort of discomfiture with the conservative movement must have addled the Bush White House. Certainly the president's venture into "Compassionate Conservatism" gives evidence of this.

In a revealing anecdote about Bush's ignorance of the conservative movement, a Bush speechwriter, Matt Latimer, himself a conservative, has recalled Bush asking him "What is this movement you keep talking about?" At the time Latimer was preparing a speech for the president to deliver at the February 2008 meeting of the Conservative Political Action Conference, an annual gathering of movement conservatives from all over the country. "Well, the conservative movement," the speechwriter explained. "You know, the one that started in the sixties, when conservative groups first took root." Responded the befuddled forty-third president, "I whupped Gary Bauer's ass in 2000."[15]

This brings me to a detail that I believe is essential to ensuring the conservatives' recovery. Conservatives must continue to see themselves as members of a self-conscious movement. Some thoughtful conservatives dissent from my position. Dan Oliver, an important movement conservative since his days as an editor at the *National Review* in the 1970s and later a member of the Reagan administration, has written, "The 'Movement' is over. Conservatives won. Conservatism is now a national intellectual and political force. To speak of conservatism today as a 'movement' belittles it, marginalizes it . . . Now we've had a generation—

a whole generation!—of deregulation, privatization, and tax cuts."[16] No less a conservative figure than George Will holds to this belief too. I disagree, and George W.'s unawareness of the conservative movement—even as he was resorting to it for policies, personnel, and votes—supports my case.

Conservatives need to continue to see themselves as members of a movement. Modern conservatism has always been about ideas that trace back to the late 1940s and the Mont Pelerin Society. The ideas were augmented in the 1950s when writers such as Frank Meyer fused the ideas of classical liberalism with those of American traditionalists. Unlike Liberalism, conservatism has not been restrictive, suffering the tendency toward extremism that Cass Sunstein has written about in *Going to Extremes: How Like Minds Unite and Divide.* There he observes the like-minded, congregated together, mouthing the same lines and intensifying their shared views.

Conservatism began with a broader base than Liberalism and a deeper respect for personal liberty. It began as an alliance of factions—the limited-government advocates, the traditionalists, the anti-Communists—and has been hospitable toward incoming groups ever since, for instance, the neoconservatives, the Reagan Democrats, and the evangelicals. Continuing as a movement embracing a diverse base, the conservatives will not be in danger of operating, say, as a political Vatican engaged in excommunicating the wayward. Moreover, continuing as a movement will serve to objectify our ideas and policies and give us—and future George W. Bushes—a sense of what conservatism is.

A movement has a better chance of identifying future Jack Abramoffs for the charlatans that they are and of responding to such preposterosities as "Heroic Conservatism."

So by maintaining ourselves as a self-conscious movement, we will not be restricting ourselves unduly. What we will do is maintain the standards by which one is judged a conservative. In the first decade of the early twenty-first century, the Republican Congress's profligate spending was anathema to limited government. Had we acted more as a movement, the profligacy might have been squelched or at least identified for the deviation from modern American conservatism that it was. Conservatism viewed as a movement will allow us authoritative voices that during the coming Conservative Revival will pronounce resoundingly who is conducting the public business as a conservative and who is not. Those voices will be able to distinguish who is, as Lady Thatcher would put it, "one of us" and who is not.

A movement provides standards and authoritative figures to offer such judgments. The voices need not be seen as infallible. The judgments need not be seen as beyond dispute. But they will create dialogue that is instructive. Without the use of the word *movement*, all the dynamism that goes with it disappears. A movement fades into an ethos and blows away. In its absence the degenerative process that Eric Hoffer warned of is made easier: soon conservatism becomes a business, then a racket. Were Hoffer around in the last years of the Bush administration, I fear he would have recognized a considerable number of racketeers, some calling themselves conservative, some claiming to be reformers (RCs). That degenerative process must be prevented. The conservatives, from their archipelago of think tanks, their magazines, their talk shows and Web sites, will set the standards. Nothing lasts forever, but by maintaining the conservative movement, we shall resist the corrosions of time, at least for a while.

Actually, since November 2008 there have been spirited public demonstrations taking place on behalf of conservative core values all over the country. There have been the Tea Party rallies. Dick Armey—himself an occasional participant—marvels that these practically spontaneous gatherings have been organized with, he says, "nobody" in charge but with hundreds of thousands of people participating.[17] There have been the independent voices ringing out at town hall meetings, where members of Congress are harangued about the need for lower taxes and limited government. All of this is broad based and pretty much in sync with a Conservative Revival, though the ever-hopeful Liberals and their friends in the media warn that a third party is in the making and an eventual conservative splintering. This variation on the conservative crack-up theme has been heard before, and it never materializes.

More highly organized have been the regular meetings of seasoned conservatives all over the country. In Washington, D.C., a broadly based group of seasoned conservative movement veterans has been meeting every Wednesday morning (at 7:30 a.m.!) since November 2008 to respond to the Obama initiatives and to charter a conservative alternative. Led by the likes of President Reagan's attorney general Ed Meese and a veteran of the Contract with America–era Congress, ex-congressman David McIntosh, this group is called the Conservative Action Project. Weekly it sends out what it calls a "Memo for the Movement" to hundreds of leaders and activists across the country. It responds to issues and nominations pending before Congress. It includes writers such as John Fund of the *Wall Street Journal* and Al Regnery of the *American Spectator*, activists such as Grover Norquist of Americans for Tax Reform and Matt Kibbe of FreedomWorks (a force behind the otherwise spontaneous Tea Parties), and think tank leaders such as Chris DeMuth (until recently president of AEI) and Ed Feulner (president of the Heritage Foundation). Meese has expressed his satisfaction over its progress in a late 2009 memo, explaining that "since the Conservative Action Project began its efforts conservatives are working together more often and quarrelling less."[18] In the memo he outlines over half a dozen "working groups" of members who represent every one of the original constituent members of the conservative movement. Conservatism that was supposed to be "dead" after the 2008 election is obviously very much alive.

Thus, as this book runs off the presses and heads for the bookstores, we see hundreds of thousands of conservatives taking the field of battle, their challenge made easier by the spirited war of ideas fought so successfully from the think tanks that F. A. Hayek and the conservative philanthropists envisaged.

Over the years much of the world that was once petrified

in collectivism and socialism now accepts—or at least recognizes—the vitality of markets and of supply-side economics. Deregulation and antitrust reform, once pioneered
by such conservative think tanks as AEI, Hoover, and the
Brookings Institution (a Liberal think tank still disciplined
by empiricism) now has a place in public policy. Welfare
reform propounded so cogently by Charles Murray in his
very successful book, *Losing Ground,* and elaborated on
within conservative think tanks (also with the involvement
of significant numbers of moderate Democratic Leadership
Council Democrats) prefigured the Welfare Reform Act of
1996. Its benefits to the poor remain convincing even as
Obama's collectivists labor to return the poor to the hopeless dependency of the Great Society. Voucherization
approaches to education and to entitlement (Social Security,
Medicare) reform have come from the archipelago of conservative think tanks—again with a tip of the hat to
Brookings. Of particular importance to the health care alternatives to ObamaCare are the policies of eliminating the tax
subsidy for employer-provided health insurance, eliminating
state "healthcare mandates," and permitting national rather
than state markets in health insurance—all are conservative
think tank projects. Even Health Savings Accounts find their
provenance at those think tanks. Finally, tort reform, a
mainstay of the Federalist Society's envisaged reforms for
the law, is another way of lowering health care costs, without following Liberalism back into the discredited world of
government-controlled health care.

There are dozens of other alternative policies circulating through public policy debates that would have been unimaginable in the immediate post–World War II world. All are the products of the conservative movement's long and honorable war of ideas. Few were available when the conservatives took on the Great Society. That they are available now as the conservatives take on Obama's collectivists is cause for optimism about the conservatives' road to recovery.

7

PLANNING TO PREVAIL

An Agenda for a
Conservative Future

The conservatives' road to recovery against the Prophet Obama's collectivists will not be boring. The country is at war with Islamofascist terrorists who on September 11, 2001, launched an even more treacherous attack than Japan's December 7, 1941, strike on Pearl Harbor. That sneak attack was contained to military and naval installations. The Islamofascists' sneak attack was, however, on unarmed private citizens, and it used commercial aircraft commandeered by enemy combatants. Such treachery presents ongoing threats to our security, as well as to our constitutional freedoms. We also face the threats of rogue nations intent on acquiring weapons of mass destruction that could present us with a new world of barbarism unforeseen by Churchill or Roosevelt or any of the other giants who contrived the durable world order that followed World War II. Finally, the country must contend with an uncertain economy that began with a serious recession and remains fragile, thanks to the prodigality of the Liberal

Democrats who responded so giddily to White House chief of staff Rahm Emanuel's bloodless maxim, "You never want a serious crisis to go to waste."[1] Their blueprint is not for a Reaganite recovery but a Perónist Argentina.

Yet conservatives' strengths today are equal to these challenges. We have a record of achievement vouchsafed for us by the Reagan Revolution. We are no longer on the fringes of politics but at the center. Our policy alternatives have been devised in our think tanks and proven by experience. We can cheerfully put forward an agenda to the American people that is compelling, offering both economic growth and national security. We should do so not out of defensiveness or peevishness but out of our shared sense of American exceptionalism and with the optimism that inheres in the Reagan legacy.

The Liberals do not believe in American exceptionalism, and the cheerfulness of earlier Liberals such as Hubert Humphrey, the Senate's "Happy Warrior," has deteriorated into anger. Liberalism is led by prigs who are embarrassed by our history and oblivious of American achievement. As the Prophet Obama told two thousand Europeans at his Strasbourg Town Hall speech on April 2, 2009, "In America, there's a failure to appreciate Europe's leading role in the world. Instead of celebrating your dynamic union and seeking to partner with you to meet common challenges, there have been times where America has shown arrogance and been dismissive, even derisive."[2] Frankly, that is an even more bizarre statement than Emanuel's apparent delight in crisis. One year into the administration of the most left-wing president in American history, it is apparent that these Liberals are something America has never witnessed at the top of American government before. They are postmodern. For them the past is a delusion and the present is a hoax.

For Obama, our first postmodern president, there is naturally no objective truth and, as we have come to apprehend from his public utterances both here and on foreign soil, no American record of splendid achievement—nothing to be especially proud of about the country he governs. He cannot conceive of America as being Ronald Reagan's "shining city upon a hill." The forty-fourth president is unimpressed by America's late-twentieth-century record of defeating Communism and creating unprecedented prosperity for all Americans, a prosperity that has even begun to reach the struggling people of the developing world. To Obama, America is a failed state, and so he has traveled the world, apologizing for the delusions that he imagines have brought so much discredit to America's brief but admirable history. Jimmy Carter was the first former president to speak ill of a sitting president while on foreign soil. Obama has surpassed Jimmy. He is the first sitting president to speak ill of *America* while on foreign soil, and he has done so repeatedly.

During his first year as America's pioneering postmodern president, he has routinely revealed his indifference to objective truth. Alas, in a world polluted by *Kultursmog*, it can be dangerous to judge him by past standards, which is to say, to accuse him of lying. Only a theretofore obscure congressman has been sufficiently brash to do so, whereupon the wretch immediately suffered widespread obloquy even from the clergy—*particularly* from the clergy. After that indiscretion the artless congressman utterly disappeared from sight. Possibly he has been consigned to a mental institution.

His indiscretion occurred during the September 9, 2009 joint session of Congress in response to the president's, shall we call it "contra-factual," appraisal of the Democrats' health care proposals. As the president put it, he would reduce health care costs by expanding health care spending, possibly by $1 trillion—postmodern to the utmost! Elsewhere in the speech, an even more notable contrafactual was heaved up, even while President Obama's government was taking over two huge automobile corporations and many large financial institutions with a $700 billion bailout. At a time when his administration was urging a $787 billion stimulus bill, a cap and trade bill that would add perhaps $800 to $2,000 to every family's tax bill, and a massive health care reform that would cost $1 trillion—possibly $2 trillion—over the next decade while extending government jurisdiction over 16 percent of the economy, Obama struck a suavely Reaganite chord. From the Speaker's rostrum, the most profligate president in American history explained that he was spilling all this red ink "not because I believe in bigger government—I don't."[3] Network news cameras broadcast the entire speech to the nation, doubling as news instrumentalities for the media and surveillance cameras for the taxpayers.

During Obama's first year in office, some of his contra-factuals have attracted polite laughter; some have attracted rude horse laughs. There was his throwaway line during a defense of his Economic Recovery and Reinvestment Act, where he cavalierly promised "to forbid the use of these funds to build things like dog parks"[4]—polite snickers. Alas, a mischievous libertarian blogger soon photographed a government-posted sign adjacent to—where else?—a dog park, and the park was just blocks from the White House. Posted on the Web site of *Reason* magazine, the sign reads, "Project Funded by The American Recovery and Reinvestment Act"—rude horse laughs![5] Some of the year's contra-factuals were simply brazen provocations. At a February 9 press conference, Obama made bold to boast of his stimulus bill: "What it does not contain, however, is a single pet project, not a single earmark." Perhaps not, as this postmodernist said, a "single" earmark, but reporters did count nine thousand![6] Is this simply postmodern math, or was that obscure congressman onto something back in February?

The Obama administration's first federal budget would metastasize federal spending from its modern-day average of around 20 percent of gross domestic product (GDP) to more than 25 percent—an unprecedented peacetime tumor. When asked by a C-SPAN interviewer, "At what point do we run out of money?" he responded glibly, "Well, we *are* out of money now. We are operating in deep deficits."[7] Yet being postmodern, he kept right on spending, aided and abetted by the collectivists in Congress. In fact, at the end of 2009, the president who had lamented,

"We *are* out of money" promised to "spend our way out of this recession."[8] The estimated bill for that outburst was put at an additional $170 billion.

In 2009 Obama and his collectivists rang up a deficit of $1.4 trillion. They did this despite the fact that the government was already facing a huge budget overhang from long-established entitlements such as Medicaid, Medicare, and Social Security. Students of public policy had been warning about this looming crisis since the late 1990s. Yet their warnings proved to be futile.*

As we have seen, a Republican Congress began the spending spree with President George W. Bush doing almost nothing to address the approaching entitlement crisis. When he left office, the 2009 budget deficit was forecast at $800 billion. Such extravagance became an issue with conservatives and with opportunistic Democrats too. Many conservatives in the last years of the Bush administration turned their backs on the Republicans. The Democratic minority exploited the Republicans' profligacy, promising frugality while transforming itself into the congressional majority in the 2006 midterm elections. Recognizing the popularity of fiscal conservatism, congresswoman Nancy Pelosi went so far as to declaim, "Democrats are committed to no deficit spending, pay-as-

---

*By the end of 2009, American unfunded liabilities and off-the-balance-sheet entitlements were three times the economy, according to the Peter G. Peterson Foundation, with Medicare and Social Security alone amounting to more than $40 trillion of commitments.

you-go. We will not heap mountains of debt onto future generations."[9]

Mark that down as another contra-factual. Speaker Pelosi's Democrats have been the Prophet Obama's willing accomplices. Even before the financial meltdown, Pelosi was calling for a $100 billion stimulus. Soon Obama was proposing a $1 trillion spending package. At the time, the Congressional Budget Office was predicting that the government was already facing a $1 trillion deficit without additional stimulus. That would be twice as much borrowing as in any post–World War II year, and the actual figure reached $1.4 trillion. By the end of 2009 the federal debt was predicted to grow at a rate of more than $1 trillion annually for the next five years, ending with a federal debt of $11.5 trillion in 2013.[10] By then the federal debt would explode to 53 percent of GDP, with projections putting it at 85 percent of GDP in 2018, 100 percent in 2022, and 200 percent in 2038.[11]

Conservatives must shout, "STOP!" Let the Reformed Conservatives devise clever stratagems for luring urban sophisticates from their yoga classes and pedicure salons to vote—what do the RCs advise—Progressive Republicanism or Heroic Conservatism, or perhaps Codswallop Conservatism? The Davidians can hold forth on the lethal consequences for Republicans, if they continue channeling Ronald Reagan at party headquarters or fail to capture the Kazak vote. Conservatives can rescue the country from a Perónist future and return to political dominance by standing by our original principles and employing the policies that revived America in the 1980s.

A Conservative agenda for our road to recovery must be based on the principles that are at the foundation of the movement. We must return to limited government and private-sector growth.

Since the Reagan administration, we have demonstrated that we have the policies for growth and national security. Beginning with the Reagan reforms, the economy entered upon a long and peaceful period of expansion. America's place in the world had not been so secure since the immediate aftermath of World War I. The period lasted a quarter of a century. Rendered nostalgic after Obama's first year of pompous posturing and reckless spending, the venerable neoconservative intellectual Charles Krauthammer recalled, "The miracle [he was referring to what he termed the "disappearance" of the Soviet Union], in major part wrought by Ronald Reagan,* bequeathed the ultimate peace dividend: a golden age of the most profound peace and prosperity."[12]

President Reagan demonstrated that government's bite into GDP lowers growth and raises unemployment. For twenty-five years prosperity spread, unemployment declined, and the federal government's percentage of GDP remained in the neighborhood of 20 percent or lower. During 2000, government spending was actually 18.35 percent of GDP. After that both parties opened the spending spigot. Since 2007,

---

*Interestingly, in the *Kultursmog* it is always Mikhail Gorbachev, the failed Russian leader, who receives top billing for the end of the Cold War, rarely Ronald Reagan, the successful American president.

with Republican spending and Democratic splurging, the federal government's annual bite out of GDP has increased to over 24 percent in 2009. The economy contracted, and unemployment topped 10 percent. That is precisely what our experience from the 1960s and 1970s indicated would take place. Moreover, at some point, unless measures are taken against it, inflation will return.

In the 1970s this was called *stagflation*. Eventually we shall have stagflation II, unless the spending is curtailed and taxes are restrained. No economically literate American should be surprised. As supply-sider Brian Wesbury has demonstrated, through the late 1960s and the unhappy decade that followed, unemployment climbed apace with government spending's growth. So did inflation, while growth stagnated.[13] To prevent the return of a Jimmy Carter economy, spending should be kept in the range of 20 percent of GDP and tax revenues at their historically optimum level of just over 18 percent.

The first priority of a Conservative agenda for recovery must be economic revival, again based on what we know works. Let us begin with budget reform, with tax reform, with health care reform, and work our way through the entitlements that should have been addressed years ago.

FINANCIAL REFORMS

BUDGET REFORM

Budget reform should include a compulsory cap on total spending to keep that spending at or below 20 percent of

GDP, the recent historic level for economic growth in the private sector. There should be a regularly scheduled congressional review of entitlement programs. If Congress surpasses its spending caps, an automatic restraint mechanism should be in place to restrain congressional extravagance. Finally, a supermajority vote by Congress should be required in the event that Congress attempts to raise tax revenue above its historically optimum level of 18.5 percent of GDP.

TAX REFORM

For my money, the best tax reform that would ensure economic growth and the benefits of increased individual freedom and privacy is Steve Forbes's flat tax, as laid out in his 2005 book, *The Flat Tax Revolution*. Briefly stated, it envisages interring, perhaps cremating, the present nine-million-word tax code with all of its impossible complexity, loopholes, unfairness, and opportunities for IRS snooping. Its place would be taken by a single-rate income and corporate tax of 17 percent. A citizen's income would be taxed only once, encouraging citizens to save and invest, thus encouraging economic growth.

Forbes argues for generous exemptions for adults and children. A family of four would pay no federal income tax on its first $46,165 of income. Adults would receive the standard tax exemption of $13,200, and adults earning less would be removed from the tax rolls. Married couples would receive a $26,400 deduction. Heads of single-parent families would get a 30 percent higher exemption in recognition of the burden they bear while raising children on their own. Families would receive a $4,000 exemption for each dependent and a refundable tax credit of $1,000 for each child age sixteen or younger.

Under the present tax code, the burden of compliance is excessive, involving vast amounts of time or expense, or both. Under the flat tax almost everyone would pay less. Such a tax cut would encourage both economic growth and increased federal tax revenue. Had a flat tax been in place in 2005, according to a study cited by Forbes, federal revenues would have increased by $56 billion by the year 2015.[14]

With a flat tax, the present army of IRS snoops could be curtailed along with the huge lobbying efforts in Washington that seek special tax treatment for vested interests and lead to unfairness and corruption.

THE DOLLAR

Its value has been sinking alarmingly, having lost 40 percent of its value since 2002. This decline is a reflection of how Washington politicians have mismanaged the budget; their prodigality has weakened the value of the dollar, which should be strong and stable. Yet there are many other factors that influence relative currency values. Chuck Brunie, chairman of the board of the *American Spectator* and chairman emeritus of the Manhattan Institute, lists seventeen different factors.

Thoughtful economists offer several suggestions for

strengthening and maintaining the dollar. Some favor the government's "talking up the value of the dollar." Others advocate pegging the dollar to gold, or a basket of commodities or a basket of foreign currencies. Milton Friedman initiated the idea of floating exchange rates, and advocated them throughout his long life. In the case of all the other recommendations, ultimately some bureaucrat decides the value of the currency. With floating exchange rates the market, not the bureaucrat, determines the rate of exchange. Moreover, it does so faster than the bureaucrat, thus adjusting rapidly—therefore more efficiently—to real conditions in the world economy. Floating exchange rates are more in accord with conservatives' overarching goals of limited government and personal freedom, plus they are a more efficient means of valuing the dollar.

SOCIAL SECURITY

Thirty years ago, suggesting a change to Social Security could have had you arrested, committed, or worse, but as evidence of the success of the conservative think tanks and their work, serious consideration has been given to several alterations to the program. Here is a modest one: preserve Social Security for Americans aged fifty-five and older, and give younger Americans the option of investing a third of their current Social Security taxes in personal retirement accounts (PRAs). Model this after the Thrift Savings Plan available to federal employees. As with HSAs, allow personal accounts to be bequeathed to the account-holder's heirs.

HEALTH CARE REFORMS

The United States spends more than two times what the average industrialized nation spends on health care, though let us remember that it is the best in the world. Moreover, the cost of health care is growing at just under 5 percent annually, a leading reason why some Americans are not insured and that Medicare and Medicaid are heading for financial ruin. A major cause for this rising cost is the federal tax code's exclusion of employer-provided health insurance. This is unfair to those who must purchase insurance with after-tax dollars. Further, it blinds consumers of employer-provided health care to the real costs of their medical expenses and puts pressure upward on health care's costs.

The solution is to be found in bringing health care to the marketplace. End the tax-deductibility of employer-provided health care. Allow every citizen, except those enrolled in Medicare or in a military health plan, to receive a refundable tax credit to purchase Health Savings Accounts (HSAs). (The key thing is that people should have a choice of plans.) This tax credit should be available not only to those who purchase HSAs. Some people, for instance, have higher medical costs, so they may prefer a more comprehensive policy. But we could encourage more widespread use of HSAs by raising the cap on the amount of money that people could put in them. Also, owners of HSAs should be allowed to purchase health insurance in any state in the country. The money should be applicable to those employer-sponsored plans still available or to any health care plan an individual or family chooses, thus allowing product competition. Unused money in each account should be rolled over to succeeding years, and whatever money remains in each account should be part of an accountholder's estate upon death.

An additional twist to this might be to allow people with HSAs to pay for their health care expenses by drawing down from a health care debit card. This would be particularly desirable for care administered through a patient's local hospital. Administering health care payments through hospitals is an innovation recently suggested by Hunt Lawrence, a New York investor and entrepreneur who has reviewed the American health care system and believes hospitals could compete successfully with insurers while offering a broader range of services. With his, admittedly ambitious reform, hospitals could simultaneously monitor a patient's bills and health conditions. Furthermore, the hospital could neatly maintain the patient's health records, which would be portable for the patient in the event of moving from one locale to another. Of course, patients would be free to change hospitals from time to time, thus introducing competition among hospitals.

Also, let us have tort reform. Reckless malpractice lawsuits account for at least half a trillion dollars in wasted health care expenses annually through jackpot lawsuits and the unnecessary tests prescribed by doctors fearful of the reach of trial lawyers.

Finally, for those who are impoverished and unable to pay for health care, let the government give them vouchers to pay for their medical expenses up to a certain amount annually.

Whatever the consequences of the Democrats' 2009 health care monstrosity, conservatives should redouble their efforts to repeal its archaic collectivist requirements in the event that they become national policy. Notwithstanding their promises to lower health care costs, the collectivists are going to increase those costs by a huge amount while reverting to government rationing and control of doctor-patient relations.

MEDICAID REFORM

Medicaid is a federal-state health care entitlement for low-income citizens. States should be able to allow low-income citizens the option of using refundable tax credits to enroll in private insurance plans rather than the present Medicaid coverage. These individuals should also be able to use the vouchers from the federal government made available in the aforementioned healthcare reform. Both can be arranged in such a way as to restrain the present upward spiral in costs.

MEDICARE REFORM

Create a program for citizens fifty-five and younger that will begin to transition Medicare into a program in which individuals are given government payments toward the purchase of private insurance. The value of the payments would be higher for those with lower incomes and greater medical needs.

Additionally, the government should dedicate more

resources to policing rampant fraud in the program, which by some estimates surpasses $100 billion a year.

The above policies in a Conservative agenda allow for the workings of the marketplace in the purchase of health care and relieve much of the cumbersome involvement of government, with its inefficiencies, intrusions of the state into private lives, and lack of cost controls. In the case of Medicaid and Medicare reforms, there would doubtless be a need for revisions, but the main points should be adhered to: HSAs, tort reform, and an end to the tax-deductibility of employer-provided healthcare.

OTHER KEY DOMESTIC POLICIES

Based on what conservatives have learned from their experience in governance over the years, the following items should also be placed on the Conservative agenda.

EDUCATION

Despite spending more per student than almost any other industrialized nation,[15] America is not getting a good return on its educational investment. Our current top-down educational approach guarantees mediocrity, and bureaucratization explains why our publicly educated students lag behind those in the rest of the industrial world. Successful reform should ensure that the current K–12 system is progressively replaced with a mix of charter schools and school vouchers determined at the state or municipal level. Conservatives should encourage that the arts and other important but non-quantifiable areas of education be reintroduced into curricula, encouraging students to be culturally literate. Courses in civics should also be stressed in American schools, as I shall elaborate on below in discussing immigration policy.

Finally, the "Catholic school advantage" should be examined and exploited. Federal policies that limit the options of states and localities should be reexamined and eliminated to ensure the greatest freedom for students.

IMMIGRATION

Legal and illegal immigrants are regarded, variously, as a threat to social and economic order and as an underserved and neglected group. Conservatives have been unnecessarily split as to how to deal with them, though on social and economic issues, many immigrants share our values.

High on our agenda must be securing our borders, both as an antiterrorist and an anticrime measure. Moreover, the rule of law must be maintained. Illegal immigrants must pay a price for breaking our laws and devaluing the immigration procedures followed by law-abiding legal immigrants. Yet once they have paid a price and, assuming that they are otherwise law-abiding, they should be extended the opportunity for citizenship. One matter that has been overlooked in dealing with immigrants and in public education in general is the value of teaching civics both to immigrants and to native-born students. No one of voting age should be ignorant of the American system of government.

JUDICIAL APPOINTMENTS

At least one aspect of the contemporary controversy between Liberals and conservatives over the judiciary is a testimony to mankind's prodigious capacity for arguing. I have in mind the dispute over whether judges should take it upon themselves to make law. Some Liberals argue that they should. Clearly, one of the fundamental elements of the Constitution, however, makes it apparent that judges should weigh the law against precedent and the Constitution while leaving the making of law to the legislative branch of government. That is Congress's obligation. That there is any argument about this is, as I say, more evidence of the species Homo sapiens' delight in quarreling.

The legal order of the United States is, as the Federalist Society proclaims in its statement of purpose, "founded on the principles that the state exists to preserve freedom, that the separation of governmental powers is central to our Constitution, and that it is emphatically the province and duty of the judiciary to say what the law is, not what it should be." In a Conservative agenda it is important to work toward selecting judges who will follow these principles. This is critical not only for federal judges but equally for state judges. State judges make most of the decisions that have an impact on the lives of ordinary Americans.

ENERGY POLICY

America must aim for what T. Boone Pickens calls "global energy security." Pickens is the very successful

Texas energy developer. He is also the author of the Pickens Plan to break America's dependence on foreign oil. America relies on other countries for almost 70 percent of our oil needs, and many of our suppliers are either fragile regimes or hostile regimes. Adopting the Pickens Plan would be a good start toward energy security. It advocates all forms of energy production, including nuclear, wind, and solar energy, but recent breakthroughs in natural gas development have put America in the heretofore unforeseen position of ending our reliance on OPEC.

In recent years natural gas has been found in abundance in the United States. In fact, we now have 2,000 trillion cubic feet of natural gas reserves—more than twice the amount of energy in Saudi oil, and enough to last us a century. Natural gas is now cheap and cleaner than oil or coal. Simply adopting the Pickens Plan's series of tax credits for the orderly replacement of diesel-powered 18-wheeler semis and other heavy-duty vehicles with natural gas-powered vehicles over a five- to seven-year period would amount to a savings of 2.5 million barrels of oil a day. That would cut our reliance on OPEC by 50 percent. Such a cut would force oil producers to negotiate the price of oil with us rather than dictate it to us. The price would come down. Our dependence would drop. We would be granted years to develop alternative energy sources.

Global energy security would strengthen our economy and enhance our national security.

NATIONAL DEFENSE

National security is the second major challenge conservatives face in the years ahead after getting domestic policy in order. Thus far the war on terror has been relatively successful. There have been no more major attacks on our soil. We have set our most dangerous terrorist enemies back on their heels. Yet the threats remain out there, and various rogue nations continue to assist the terrorists even as they acquire weapons of mass destruction for their own use or for the use of those barbarians who lurk in the shadows. The Prophet Obama's dulcet rhetoric has been futile. Our intelligence capacity must be strengthened, and our defense capabilities maintained.

Finally there is the question of safeguarding American liberties in an era of homeland security.

HOMELAND SECURITY AND PERSONAL FREEDOMS

We know that there prowl within the borders of the United States terrorists—both American citizens and foreigners—communicating with their leaders here and abroad. Our intelligence services must monitor them. The Fourth Amendment's protections against "unreasonable searches and seizures" must be respected. Yet in gray areas, such as telecommunications transfers and airport screenings, where technology changes rapidly, government surveillance must err on the side of vigilance. During previous wars that has been the practice, and in every case constitutional protections that were abridged have been restored with the country's return to peace. That should be our policy today. We cannot hazard another 9/11.

ENHANCING INTELLIGENCE GATHERING AND ANALYSIS

I agree with the great British historian Paul Johnson. Discussing intelligence is like discussing a mystery novel whose last chapter has yet to be written. Few people, and very few laymen, can discuss intelligence with certitude.

Bill Casey, President Reagan's head of CIA, was a friend and mentor. He and I visited frequently when he was at Langley. He always said that his was the best job in Washington, but I am not so sure that he would say that today. Some say the CIA is laden in impenetrable bureaucracies, and now under President Obama, probably as risk-adverse as it was following the Church Committee hearings of the 1970s. Whether this is true or not, Johnson and I will have to await the writing of a last chapter.

There does seem to be emerging an intelligent consensus that all our varied intelligence organizations suffer from a lack of what was instituted in the military in the aftermath of hearings held by Senator Barry Goldwater and Congressman Bill Nicholas in the 1980s, namely, "jointness." What it has meant is that all branches of the armed forces operate in a way that integrates resources, planning, communications, and everything else that composes a method to dominate any battlefield.

Jointness needs to be adopted by our intelligence organizations from CIA to NSA to Homeland Security and including all the bureaucracies in between so that they are required to integrate in the same manner. Conservatives should call for congressional hearings similar to those over which Goldwater and Nicholas presided in their day to ensure that maximum cooperation exists in the gathering and analysis of intelligence both foreign and domestic.

As we have been aware since 9/11, there are terrorists on our soil, communicating with brutal handlers from afar. The integration of intelligence agencies whose jurisdiction is domestic (FBI) with those whose jurisdiction is beyond our borders (CIA, NSA) is crucial to American security.

MAINTAINING NATIONAL DEFENSE

During the Reagan administration our national defense was regularly calibrated to the challenges the nation faced. The process adopted for that purpose was called "Defense Guidance." It followed three steps. The first entailed gauging the intentions and capabilities of enemies or potential enemies. The second reviewed available weaponry, manpower to use the weaponry, and the attendant costs in executing a mission with the selected weaponry and manpower. In the third step, to whatever extent there might be a mismatch between the results from the first step and the second step, the Pentagon would build or recruit whatever was needed to fill the gap. In the event of accumulated surpluses, they would be cut or retired.

At the height of President Reagan's rearmament, defense expenditures were 6.2 percent of GDP. Facing the present threats against us, we do not need to maintain such levels of military spending. The defense budget now stands at 4.8 percent of GDP and is projected to drop to 3 percent. That last figure is too low. Conservatives must favor maintaining our military as the most powerful in the world.

Finally, I would be remiss if I did not place on the Conservative agenda what I modestly unveiled some years ago as the Tyrrell Doctrine. During the Iraq War, divisions developed among conservatives over whether it is in our national interest to spread democracy to foreign lands. Some conservatives argued that it is the humane thing to do. Further, it is in our national interest because democracies tend to be more peaceful than dictatorships. Other conservatives argued that it is a futile pursuit and a waste of American blood and treasure. I side with the latter, as did neoconservative Jeane Kirkpatrick. Contrary to the critics, this is not necessarily a split between neoconservatives and earlier varieties of conservatives. Rather, it is a question of how best to maintain our national interest. Jeane and I supported swatting the dictator but not endeavoring to teach the Iraqis civics. I like to think that she, a member of the *American Spectator*'s board of directors, was an early advocate of the Tyrrell Doctrine.

The Tyrrell Doctrine recognizes that it is too costly and difficult to plant democracy on the unwelcoming soil of countries that have no sympathy for it, for instance, Iraq or Afghanistan. It would be better to warn brutes such as the late Saddam Hussein or the now fugitive Al-Qaeda leaders against threatening our interests or our allies. If they fail to get the hint, send in our forces to bust the place up. Then leave. After we flattened Iraq it was obvious that tyrants throughout the region got the message. The Lebanese, the Libyans, the Syrians, and even the obnoxious Iranian mullahs instantaneously became agreeable, almost docile. The problem is that we remained in Iraq, trying to evangelize democracy and apparently transform Iraqi womenfolk into feminists, which, given the irascible nature of Iraqis, would make the maintenance of public order impossible. We should have left the place in a heap.

AMERICAN EXCEPTIONALISM

This brings me to a final item on the Conservative agenda, American exceptionalism.

We should be proud and confident of it. Andrew Roberts, the great British historian, reminds us of Churchill's response to the Great Depression: "I do not think America is going to smash," Churchill told Bernard Baruch, his American stockbroker. "On the contrary I believe that they will quite soon begin to recover . . . they carved it out of the prairie and the forests. They are going to have a strong national resurgence in the near future." Churchill, of course, was half-American, so not surprisingly, Roberts reminds us, Churchill believed "in the massive regenerative power of the United States," which "was a constant in his life. He believed that given the will, Americans could achieve anything because America was special."[16] What prompted Andrews to write this was his fear that the Obama Democrats are causing some Americans to doubt our exceptionalism.

Conservatives should be heartened by our country's exceptional character and role in recent history. We should inspire our fellow citizens with their country's exceptionalism, for as Roberts notes, it is under fire from the American Left.

Believing in American exceptionalism is not a recent or provincial American conceit. As Charles Murray observed in his 2009 Irving Kristol lecture:

> American exceptionalism is not just something that Americans claim for themselves. Historically, Americans have been different as a people, even peculiar, and everyone around the world has recognized it. I'm thinking of qualities such as American optimism even when there doesn't seem to be any good reason for it. That's quite uncommon among the peoples of the world. There is the striking lack of class envy in America—by and large, Americans celebrate others' success instead of resenting it. That's just about unique, certainly compared to European countries, and something that drives European intellectuals crazy. And then there is perhaps the most important symptom of all, the signature of American exceptionalism—the assumption by most Americans that they are in control of their own destinies. It is hard to think of a more inspiriting quality for a population to possess, and the American population still possesses it to an astonishing degree. No other country comes close.[17]

There are two historic images that have through the decades reminded us of our exceptionalism. The first is that of "a city upon a hill," so often identified with President Ronald Reagan, though John F. Kennedy was the first president to invoke this ideal of our nation's earliest settlers, in a speech in Massachusetts in 1961. For both men America was to be a moral force, observable to the world.

The second image is that of the frontier, to which Churchill alluded when he told Baruch, "They carved it out of the prairie and the forests." It was the subject of Frederick Jackson Turner's paper delivered to the American Historical Association in 1893. From the conquest of the frontier, Turner believed Americans developed a special character that separated them from what he called "Old Europe," and made Americans inquisitive, practical, inventive, restless, and "powerful to effect great ends." Conquering the frontier made us strong and individualistic.[18] It made us unique, and as part of a Conservative agenda, we should recognize our uniqueness.

AFTERWORD

For Real Hope and Change

Throughout this book I have posited a series of observations provoked by the perdurable claim made once again in 2008 by Liberalism's coroners that conservatism is suffering rigor mortis. Calmly, I have observed that the conservative corpse has risen again. Then I observed the repeated death notices that Liberalism received, beginning with the triumphs of Ronald Reagan. I based these and subsequent observations on solid news accounts, polling data, and simple acts of logical deduction. I have also posited several of my carefully arrived-at theses about contemporary politics, which I hope are at once instructive and amusing.

My thesis about *Kultursmog* is fundamental to understanding the American political condition and the state of conservatism. An awareness of the Liberals' domination of American culture has been abroad in the land since November 13, 1969, when a recent convert to conservatism, Vice President Spiro T. Agnew, first raised the issue to a national audience during a speech in Des Moines, Iowa. Interestingly, the discourse was written by a Nixon speechwriter, Pat Buchanan. As you might expect, Liberal media apparatchiks denied everything; but they did begin their self-conscious practice of opening an "opinion page" to writers dissenting from the Liberal orthodoxy. The *New York Times* even invited a speechwriter from the Nixon White House, William Safire, to become a *Times* columnist. Since then the *Kultursmog* has remained untreated. Its presence explains another of my theses, the marginalization of conservatives even in time of conservative preponderance, for instance, during the Reagan 1980s, the Gingrich Congress, and the presidency of George W. Bush.

This marginalization is not only caused by the unwelcoming gases of the *Kultursmog*. It is also caused by my thesis regarding a fundamental difference between conservatives and Liberals. Namely, the conservative political libido is restrained by comparison to the Liberals' political libido, which is positively inclement. Thus the conservatives' political failings are often the product of inaction, while the Liberals' are the product of hyperactivity. The consequence of *Kultursmog* and of the profound difference between the political instinct of the conservative and that of the Liberal is that conservatives manifest what anthropologists identify as "crab antics." Crabs at the bottom of a bucket, when the bucket is tipped, pull each other back in the scramble to reach the top. Conservatives pull each other back too. That might explain why so few high-quality leaders are recognizable among conservative intellectuals and politicians. As I hope I have made clear, they are out there.

Lack of leadership in the years ahead does not worry me. Doubtless, leaders will step forward. I remember Ronald Reagan's brief campaign in 1968, his more successful campaign in 1976, and his election in 1980. In each election I did my small bit. Not all conservatives shared my confidence in him. His manifest talents eluded them. Yet, at least during those early years of the conservative movement, we did not have to overcome problems that accumulated during George W. Bush's presidency, when, as Eric Hoffer once anticipated, a "great cause" descended into a "business" and then into a "racket." The Bush 43 years witnessed the arrival of the conservative hustler. Sometimes the hustlers were crooks, such as Jack Abramoff. Other times they were the intellectual opportunists who thought they could advance in the *Kultursmog* by tut-tutting established members of the conservative movement. I have in mind the Reformed Conservatives, the Davidians, and the occasional mini-cons.

Fortunately, as has happened every time conservatism has plateaued and subsided, from 1964 on, conservatism recovers and comes back stronger. Meanwhile Liberalism, having episodically given itself over to its raving passions, appalls the average American voter and enjoys ever briefer periods in office. Today, after nearly a half century of these oscillations, conservatism is the most popular political designation in the country, outpolling even moderates, and outnumbering Liberals by two to one. If the process continues, as I predict it will, the Liberals' popularity will eventually be on a par with that that of the American Prohibition Party (PRO). Even nudists will be more numerous, particularly in California.

What is hastening this decline is not only the Liberals' propensity for immoderation but also the *Kultursmog*'s threat from what I have called New Media, which is to say, the rising conservative counterculture. Talk radio, cable talk shows, the Internet, the established conservative think tanks, and magazines of the conservative movement, are all flourishing and presenting compelling personalities armed with the tried-and-true ideas of the conservative movement. Fox News alone brings in more revenue than the combined revenues of CNN, MSNBC, and the evening news broadcasts of the networks, ABC, CBS, and NBC[1]—all reliable smokestacks of the *Kultursmog*. *Time*, *Newsweek*, the *New York Times*, and the *Washington Post* are likewise financially fragile.

With this shift it is going to be ever more difficult for the RCs and the Davidians to exploit the *Kultursmog* and make names for themselves. David Frum has almost completely slipped from sight and will have to jump off Washington's Memorial Bridge to get attention. David Brooks already has.

Recall his suicidal interview with the *New Republic*. Ingratiating himself to the Prophet Obama, he told the *New Republic*'s interviewer, "I don't want to sound like I'm bragging, but usually when I talk to senators, while they may know a policy area better than me, they generally don't know political philosophy better than me. I got the sense that he knew *both* better than me." The occasion was Brooks's first interview with Obama, then a senator with a month or so of experience on the job. Brooks went on to say, "I remember distinctly an image—we were sitting on his couches, and I was looking at his pant leg and his perfectly creased pant, and I'm thinking, (a) he's going to be president and (b) he'll be a very good president." What would this precious Washington insider have reported to the *New Republic* if Senator Obama had been wearing panty hose?

When Brooks allowed these observations in August 2009, Obama was declining in the polls and proceeding from pratfall to pratfall. My guess is his pants were already pretty well wrinkled. Yet Brooks slobbered on, proclaiming, "My overall view is ninety-five percent of the decisions they [Obama and his administration] make are good and intelligent . . . Obama sees himself as a Burkean. He sees his view of the world as a view that understands complexity and the organic nature of change."[2] Possibly there was a Burke in the Fabian Society.

Viewed from the perspective of history, the Liberals have been in a long, slow, but apparently unavoidable decline since the 1960s, when for them history stopped. From their excesses in the early Obama administration, it is clear that they completely missed the 1980s and 1990s. They have become fantasists. They believe all the legends they have created for themselves. As one after another is defeated at the polls, it might be difficult to get them to vacate their offices. Special counselors may have to be called in.

America's political center is now a center shaped by conservatism. With the growth of the conservative counterculture, the prospects are good for conservatism now to do what it should have done in the 1980s and act not merely like a political party but like a political culture. Finally, the conservatives can stop pulling each other back. They stand poised to create what the New Deal created, a New Order. History rarely repeats itself, but it does occasionally approximate itself.

NOTES

INTRODUCTION
1. Sir William Harcourt quoted in Harold Cox, *Economic Liberty* (Charleston, SC: BiblioLife, 2009), 170.
2. William F. Buckley Jr., *Up from Liberalism* (New York: McDowell, Obolensky Inc., 1959), xiv.

CHAPTER 1
1. Ethan Bronner, *Battle for Justice: How the Bork Nomination Shook America* (New York: Norton, 1989), 98.
2. *Facts on File 1987* (New York: Facts on File, 1987), 738.
3. Bronner, *Battle for Justice*, 295.
4. Dan Spencer, "Most Think Obama Believes in Bigger Government," *Examiner* (Nashville), March 5, 2009, http://www.examiner.com/x-268-Right-Side-Politics-Examiner~y2009m3d5-Most-think-Obama-believes-in-bigger-government.
5. Charles Krauthammer, "The Conservative Crackup," *Washington Post*, September 22, 1989.
6. William Jefferson Clinton, U.S. Capitol, Washington DC. State of the Union address, January 23, 1996, http://clinton4.nara.gov/WH/New/other/sotu.html.
7. John Bartlett, *Bartlett's Familiar Quotations*, 17th ed., Justin Kaplan, ed. (New York: Brown & Little, 2002).
8. Lee Walczak, "How Bush Outwitted the Dems," *Business*

Week, November 8, 2002, http://www.businessweek.com/bwdaily
/dnflash/nov2002/nf2002118_3711.htm.

9. Jonah Goldberg, "Cracked," *National Review Online*,
March 30, 2005, http://nationalreview.com/gold-berg/goldberg2005
03300801.asp.

10. Ibid.

11. Ibid.

12. Eric Hoffer, *The True Believer: Thoughts on the Nature
of Mass Movements* (New York: Perennial [HarperCollins], 1989).

13. Arthur M. Schlesinger Jr., *A Life in the Twentieth
Century: Innocent Beginnings, 1917–1950* (New York: Houghton
Mifflin Company, 2000).

14. Noel Annan, *Our Age: Portrait of a Generation* (London:
George Weidenfeld and Nicolson, 1990).

15. Patrick J. Buchanan, "The Apologists," *American
Conservative*, January 27, 2003.

16. Goldberg, "Cracked."

17. Jonah Goldberg, "Cloudy Fortunes for Conservatism,"
Washington Post, January 13, 2008.

18. R. Emmett Tyrrell, "A Hillary in Your Cabinet,"
Washington Times, December 5, 2008, http://www.washington
times.com/news/2008/dec/05/a-hillary-in-your-cabinet/.

19. John Kerry, (statement before the Senate Foreign
Relations Committee, April 22, 1971), quoted in part in Mackubin
Thomas Owens, "Vetting the Vet Record," *National Review*
online, January 27, 2004, http://www .nationalreview.com/owens
/owens200401270825.asp. See entire text at https://facultystaff
.richmond.edu/~ebolt /history398 /JohnKerryTestimony.html.

20. Editorial, "Dimmest Bulb of 2008 – Sen. Joe Biden,"
Washington Examiner, Opinion, December 28, 2008,
http://www.washingtonexaminer.com/opinion/Dimmest_Bulb_of
_2008_-_Sen_Joe_Biden.html.

21. Associated Press, "Joe Biden: I am a hard coal miner,"
Chicago Sun-Times, October 1, 2008.

22. Ibid.

23. Kirsten Powers, "Biden's Bungles: A Blatant Bias," *New
York Post*, October 29, 2009.

24. *Lou Dobbs Show*, CNN, October 16, 2008.

25. Mark Leibovich, "Meanwhile the Other No. 2 Keeps On Punching," *New York Times,* September 19, 2008.

26. R. Emmett Tyrrell Jr., *Boy Clinton: The Political Biography* (Washington DC: Regnery, 1996), 49.

27. Already at least one biographer has come up with evidence that the book was written by Obama's Chicago friend, the 1960s radical Bill Ayers. See Christopher Andersen's *Barack and Michelle: Portrait of an American Marriage* (New York: William Morrow, 2009), 162–67.

28. Charles Krauthammer, "The Campaign Autopsy," *Washington Post,* November 7, 2008.

CHAPTER 2

1. Lydia Saad, "Conservatives Finish 2009 as No. 1 Ideological Group," Gallup Poll, January 7, 2010.

2. Ross Douthat, "When Buckley Met Reagan," *New York Times Book Review*, January 18, 2009.

3. Frank Meyer, "Conservatism and Republican Candidates," *National Review*, December 12, 1967.

4. Jeffrey M. Jones. "Republicans Edge Ahead of Democrats in 2010 Vote," Gallup, November 11, 2009, http://www.gallup .com/poll/124226/republicans-edge-ahead -democrats-2010-vote .aspx.

5. Geoffrey Norman, "The Godfather of Neoconservatism (and his family)," *Esquire Fortnightly*, January 30, 1979, 131.

6. Ross Douthat, "Race 2020," *New York Times*, July 20, 2009.

7. John Bresnahan and Manu Raju, "Jeff Sessions Is the GOP's New Point Man," *Politico*, May 6, 2009.

8. David Frum, *The Right Man: The Surprising Presidency of George W. Bush* (New York: Random House, 2003), 275.

9. David Frum, *Comeback: Conservatism That Can Win Again* (New York: Broadway, 2009), 8.

10. David Brooks, interview by *Atlantic Monthly*, October 6, 2008.

11. David Brooks, "Darkness at Dusk," *New York Times*, November 11, 2008.

12. Jones, "Republicans Edge Ahead of Democrats in 2010 Vote."

13. Sean Wilentz, *The Age of Reagan: A History, 1974–2008* (New York: Harper, 2008), 92.

14. Ibid., 268.

15. "Read 'Em and Weep," CBS News, December 14, 2000.

16. Ibid.

17. Lee Walczak, "How Bush Outwitted the Dems," *Business Week*, November 8, 2002, http://www.businessweek.com/bwdaily/dnflash/nov2002/nf2002118_3711.htm.

18. Adam Nagourney, "The 2004 Election: The Losing Party; Baffled in Loss, Democrats Seek Road Forward," *New York Times*, November 7, 2004.

19. Ibid.

20. Kathy Kiely and Mimi Hall, "Losses Leave Dems Pondering the Future," *USAToday*.com, November 3, 2004.

21. Ibid.

22. Nagourney, "The 2004 Election."

23. Sam Tanenhaus, "Conservatism Is Dead: An Intellectual Autopsy," *New Republic*, February 18, 2009; Sam Tanenhaus, *The Death of Conservatism* (New York: Random House, 2009).

CHAPTER 3

1. David Frost interview with William F. Buckley Jr., PBS, June 28, 1996.

2. Adam Bellow, *World Affairs*, Summer 2008, 28.

3. William F. Buckley, Jr. "Did He Kiss Joe?" *National Review Online*, July 5, 2006. http://article .nationalreview.com/?q=NGEwNmYxYjRhZmRkZjA4MmM1YzE5MDIzMzJlYjExNmU=.

4. Helen Kennedy, "The joke's on Mr. Morality: Bennett's slot woes may make virtue a tough sell," *Daily News*, May 11, 2003, http://www.nydailynews.com/archives/news/2003/05/11/2003-05-11_the_joke_s_on_mr __morality__.html.

5. Author interview with Al Regnery, July 18, 2009.

6. Henry Kissinger, eulogy for William F. Buckley Jr., New York, April 4, 2008. http://www.henryakissinger.com/eulogies /040408.html.

7. Ibid.

8. Christopher Buckley "Sorry, Dad, I'm Voting for Obama," *Daily Beast*, October 10, 2008, http://www.the daily-

beast.com/ blogs-and-stories/2008-10-10/the-conservative-case-for
-obama/full/.

9. Christopher Buckley, "My Brush with Rush," *Daily Beast*, October 27, 2008, http://www.thedailybeast .com/blogs-and
-stories/2008-10-27/my-brush-with-rush.

10. Christopher Buckley, *Losing Mum and Pup: A Memoir* (New York: Twelve, Hachette Book Group, 2009), 82.

11. Christopher Buckley, "A Eulogy for My Father," *National Review Online*, April 4, 2008.

12. Ibid.

13. Buckley, *Losing Mum and Pup*, 28.

14. Alfred S. Regnery, *Upstream: The Ascendance of American Conservatism* (New York: Threshold Editions, 2008), 64.

15. Ibid., 110–13.

16. John B. Judis, *William F. Buckley, Jr.: Patron Saint of the Conservatives* (New York: Simon & Schuster, 1988), 372.

17. Richard Brookhiser, *Right Time, Right Place: My Coming of Age with William F. Buckley Jr. and the Conservative Movement* (New York: Basic Books, 2009), 121.

18. Jeane Kirkpatrick, "Dictatorships and Double Standards," *Commentary*, November 1979.

19. Tevi Troy, *Intellectuals and the American Presidency: Philosophers, Jesters, or Technisions? 1960 to Present* (Lanham, MD: Rowman & Littlefield, 2003), 110.

20. Brookhiser, *Right Time, Right Place*, 83.

21. Jacob Burckhardt, *Reflections on History* (Indianapolis: Liberty Classics/Liberty Fund, Inc., 1979), 337.

22. Author interview with Herb London, August 13, 2009.

23. Letter from William F. Buckley Jr. to the author, October 23. 1986.

24. Sean Rowe, "With Speed (and Money) to Burn," *Broward/Palm Beach New Times*, December 31, 1998, http://www .browardpalmbeach.com/1998-12-31/news /with-speed-and-money
-to-burn/.

CHAPTER 4

1. John Milton, "Lycidas," Line 71.

---

2. Lance Morrow, Johanna McGeary, Simmons Fentress, "Nation: Is There Life After Disaster?" *Time*, November 18, 1980.

3. William Jefferson Clinton, State of the Union Address, January 23, 1996, http://clinton4.nara.gov/WH /New/other/sotu .html.

4. Lydia Saad, "'Conservatives' Are Single-Largest Ideological Group," Gallup, June 15, 2009, http://www .gallup .com/poll/120857/Conservatives-Single-Largest-Ideological-Group .aspx.

5. Lydia Saad, "Conservatives Maintain Edge as Top Ideological Group," Gallup, October 26, 2009, http://www .gallup.com/poll/123854/conservatives-maintain-edge-top-ideological -group.aspx.

6. Cass R. Sunstein, *Going to Extremes: How Like Minds Unite and Divide* (New York: Oxford University Press, 2009), 124.

7. Author interview with James Piereson, August 19, 2009.

8. Sally C. Pipes, *The Top Ten Myths of American Health Care* (San Francisco: Pacific Research Institute, 2009), 33–39.

9. The Alger Hiss Story, http://homepages.nyu.edu/~th15 /history.html. His comments were also reprinted in a review of Oliver Stone's "Nixon," in the March 1996 issue of the American Historical Association's *Perspectives* magazine, now available at http://www.historians.org /perspectives/issues/1996/9603/9603fil1 .cfm.

10. Ibid.

11. John Ehrman, "A Half-Century of Controversy: The Alger Hiss Case," CIA, May 8, 2007, https://www.cia.gov/library /center-for-the-study-of-intelligence/kent-csi/docs/v44i5a01p.htm.

12. David Maraniss, "First Lady Launches Counterattack," *Washington Post*, January 8, 1998, http://www.washingtonpost .com/wp-srv/politics/special /clinton/stories/hillary012898.htm.

13. Dan Keating and Dan Balz, "Florida Recounts Would Have Favored Bush," *Washington Post*, November 12, 2001, http://www.washingtonpost.com /ac2/wp-dyn?pagename=article &node=&contentId =A12623-2001Nov11&notFound=true.

14. "Media Recount: Bush Won," Online *NewsHour*, April 3, 2001, http://www.pbs.org/newshour/media /media_watch/jan -june01/recount_4-3.html.

15. Clemente Lisi, "Hillary Utters Gaffe Regarding 2000 Election During Nigeria Visit," *New York Post*, August 13, 2009.

16. Charles A. Duelfer, *Hide and Seek: The Search for Truth in Iraq* (New York: PublicAffairs, 2009).

17. Calculations derived from the Bureau of Labor Statistics Web site, http://www.bls.gov/lpc/#data.

18. Calculations derived from the Office of Management and Budget, http://www.whitehouse.gov /omb/budget/Historicals/.

19. Data can be found on the Bureau of Labor Statistics Web site, where you can extract and graph the data: http://data.bls.gov /PDQ/outside.jsp?survey=ln.

20. Richard Hofstadter, "The Paranoid Style in American Politics," *Harper's Magazine*, November 1964, 77–86, http://karws.gso.uri.edu/jfk/conspiracy_theory/the_paranoid_mentality /the_paranoid_style.html.

21. "William F. Buckley Jr.," *New York Sun*, February 28, 2008.

22. Adam Meyerson, "Mr. Kaplan, Tear Down This Wall," *Policy Review*, Fall 1993, 4.

23. Ibid.

24. Author interview with Adam Meyerson, August 23, 2009.

25. Steven V. Roberts, "Washington in Transition; Reagan's Final Rating Is Best of Any President Since 40's," *New York Times*, January 18, 1989, http://www.nytimes.com/1989/01/18/us /washington-transition-reagan-s-final-rating-best-any-president -since-40-s.html.

26. R. W. Apple, "Party in the Spotlight: News Analysis; A Vulnerable Incumbent, a Limping Bush Arrives at the Convention Without Reagan's 1984 Aura of Inevitability," *New York Times*, August 18, 1992, http://www.nytimes.com/1992/08/18/news/party- spotlight-analysis-vulnerable-incumbent-limping-bush-arrives -convention.html.

27. Jill Abramson, "Image of Anita Hill Brighter in Hindsight, Galvanizes Campaigns," *Wall Street Journal*, October 5, 1992.

28. John Omicinski, cited in Don van Natta, *First Off the Tee: Presidential Hackers, Duffers, and Cheaters from Taft to Bush* (New York: Public Affairs, 2003), 185.

29. Van Natta, *First Off the Tee*, 185.

30. Adrian Wooldridge and John Micklethwait *The Right Nation: Conservative Power in America* (New York: Penguin, 2004), 107.

31. Steven M. Gillon, *The Pact* (New York: Oxford University Press, 2008), 112.

32. Terry McAuliffe with Steve Kettmann, *What a Party! My Life Among Democrats: Presidents, Candidates, Donors, Activists, Alligators, and Other Wild Animals* (New York: St. Martin's Press, 2008), 58.

33. Robert Barnes, Michael A. Fletcher, and Kevin Merida, "Justice Thomas lashes out in memoir" September 29, 2007, http://www.washingtonpost.com/wp-dyn/ content/article/2007/09/28 /AR2007092801634.html.

34. Michael Fletcher and Kevin Merida, *Supreme Discomfort: The Divided Soul of Clarence Thomas* (New York: Broadway Books, 2007).

35. William Grimes, "The Justice Looks Back and Settles Old Scores," *New York Times*, October 10, 2007, http://www.nytimes.com/2007/10/10/books/10grim.html.

36. Chris Arabia, "Jesse Jackson Exposed," *Front Page*, December 9, 2002, http://www.frontpagemag.com/readArticle.aspx?ARTID=20782, last viewed on September 17, 2009.

37. Author interview with Adam Meyerson, August 23, 2009.

38. Donald Spoto, *Jacqueline Bouvier Kennedy Onassis: A Life* (New York: St. Martin's Press, 2000), 181.

39. Arthur Meier Schlesinger, *A Thousand Days: John F. Kennedy in the White House* (New York: Houghton Mifflin, 1965), 732.

40. Author interview with Herb London, September 10, 2009

41. Douthat, "Race 2020, *New York Times*, July 20, 2009."

42. Christopher Buckley "Sorry, Dad, I'm Voting for Obama," *Daily Beast*, October 10, 2008.

43. Howard Kurtz, "Beck and the Mainstream," *Washington Post*, September 14, 2009.

44. Jim Piereson, e-mail message to author, September 14, 2009.

45. Tucker Carlson, "What I Sold at the Revolution," *New Republic*, June 9, 1997, 15.

46. Howard Kurtz, "Carlson-Norquist: Feud for Thought," *Washington Post*, July 22, 1997.

CHAPTER 5

1. Arthur M. Schlesinger Jr., "The New Conservatism: Politics of Nostalgia," *Reporter*, June 16, 1955, 9–12. Reproduced in *The Politics of Hope and The Bitter Heritage: American Liberalism in the 1960s* (Princeton: Princeton University Press, 2007), 94–104. The "afterglow" dismissal is on page 95.

2. Ibid., 99.

3. George H. Nash, *The Conservative Intellectual Movement in America: Since 1945* (New York: Basic Books, 1976), 132.

4. Ibid.

5. Ibid.

6. Jimmy Carter, commencement speech at the University of Notre Dame, Indiana, June 1997.

7. Jeane Kirkpatrick, address at Republic National Convention, Dallas, Texas, August, 1984. http://www.cnn.com /ALLPOLITICS/1996/conventions/san.diego/facts/GOP.speeches .past/84.kirkpatrick.shtml.

8. R. F. Winch, ed., *Macaulay's Essays on William Pitt, Earl of Chatham* (Charleston, SC: BiblioBazaar, 2008), 53.

9. Lewis Coser and Irving Howe, "The Role of Ideology," in Michael Curtis, ed., *Marxism: the Inner Dialogues* (Edison, NJ: Transaction Books, 1997), 34.

10. George Jean Nathan, *Monks Are Monks* (New York: Alfred A. Knopf, 1929), 116.

11. Thomas Fleming, *The New Dealer's War: FDR and the War Within World War II* (New York: Basic Books, 2002), 197; the quotation is from Fleming's text.

12. Herbert Romerstein and Eric Breindel, *The Venona Secrets: Exposing Soviet Espionage and America's Traitors* (Washington, D.C.: Regnery Publishing, Inc., 2000), 126.

13. David Reynolds, *America, Empire of Liberty: A New History of the United States* (New York: Basic Books, 2009), 324.

14. Ibid., 324–25.

15. Eric Pianin, "A Senator's Shame," *Washington Post*, June 19, 2005.

16. Betty Glad, *Jimmy Carter: In Search of the Great White House* (New York: W. W. Norton & Company, 1980), 135. For Carter's own past racism, see Steven F. Hayward, *The Real Jimmy Carter: How Our Worst Ex-President Undermines American Foreign Policy, Coddles Dictators and Created the Party of Clinton and Kerr* (Washington, DC: Regnery, 2004). A good summary is provided by David Freddoso, "Jimmy Carter's racist campaign of 1970," *Washington Examiner*, September 16, 2009, http://www.washingtonexaminer.com/opinion /blogs/beltway-confidential /Jimmy-Carters-racist-campaign-of-1970-59499482.html.

17. Michael Oakeshott, *Rationalism in Politics* (New York: Basic Books, 1962), 168.

18. Ibid.

19. Ibid., 169.

20. Ibid., 168.

21. Ibid., 169.

22. Frank S. Meyer, *In Defense of Freedom: A Conservative Credo* (Chicago: Henry Regnery Company, 1962), 1.

23. Ibid., 10.

24. Ibid., 23.

25. Ibid., 166.

26. "The Recrudescent American," by Frank S. Meyer, in William F. Buckley Jr., ed., *Did You Ever See a Dream Walking: American Conservative Thought in the Twentieth Century* (Indianapolis and New York: The Bobbs-Merrill Company, 1970), 80–83.

CHAPTER 6

1. F. A. Hayek, *The Road to Serfdom* (Chicago, the University of Chicago Press, 1994), xxxv–xxxvi.

2. James Piereson, "Investing in Conservative Ideas," Opinion archives, *Wall Street Journal*, May 27, 2005, http://www.opinionjournal.com/extra/?id=110006723.

3. F. A. Hayek, "The Intellectuals and Socialism," *University of Chicago Law Review* (Spring 1949), 417–20, 421–23, 425–33; reprinted in George B. de Huszar, ed., *The Intellectuals: A Controversial Portrait* (Glencoe, IL: Free Press, 1960), 371–84.

4. Hayek, "The Intellectuals and Socialism."

5. James Piereson, "Investing in Conservative Ideas," *Commentary*, May 2005, 52

6. Ibid., 50.

7. Tamar Lewin, "3 Conservative Foundations Are in the Throes of Change," *New York Times*, May 20, 2001, 20.

8. Robert G. Kaiser and Ira Chinoy, "Scaife: Funding Father of the Right," *Washington Post*, May 2, 1999, http://www.washingtonpost.com/wp-srv/politics /special/clinton/stories /scaifemain050299.htm.

9. Niccolo Machiavelli, *The Prince*, chap. 22, available online at http://www.classicreader.com/book/873/.

10. See for example Karen Rothmyer, "The Man Behind the Mask," *Salon.com*, April 7, 1998, http://www.salon.com/news /1998/04/07news.html; and Murray Waas, "Clinton's 'Soviet Connection,'" *Salon.com*, April 7, 1998, http://www.salon.com /news/1998/04/07newsb.html.

11. Piereson, "Investing in Conservative Ideas," *Commentary*, 49.

12. Ibid.

13. Ibid., 50.

14. Author interview with Ed Gillespie, the White House, May 8, 2008.

15. Matthew Latimer, *Speech*less: Tales of a White House Survivor* (New York: Crown, 2009), 250.

16. Daniel Oliver, "Alphaomegaizing the Conservative Movement," *American Spectator*, March 2010.

17. "Culture etc." *Washington Times*, December 4, 2009.

18. Edwin Meese III, Conservative Action Project memo, Washington, D.C., December 10, 2009.

CHAPTER 7

1. Jonathan Weisman, "Wider U.S. Interventions Would Yield Winners/Losers as Industries Realign," *Wall Street Journal*, November 20, 2008, http://online.wsj.com /article/SB12271437426 0443023.html.

2. "In Obama's Words," *The Washington Post*, April 3, 2009, http://projects.washingtonpost.com/obama-speeches/speech /123/.

3. Lynn Sweet, "Obama's speech Before Joint Session of

Congress," *Chicago Sun-Times*, February 24, 2009, http://blogs
.suntimes.com/sweet/2009/02/obmas_speech_before_joint_ses.html.

4. Foon Rhee, "Obama Nixes Own Stimulus Project,"
Political Intelligence, Boston.com, March 20, 2009, http://www
.boston.com/news/politics/politicalintelligence/2009/03/obama
_nixes_own.html.

5. Katherine Mangu-Ward, "Stimulus Goes to the Dogs,"
Reason, "Hit & Run" blog, November 18, 2009, http://reason
.com/blog/2009/11/18/stimulus-goes-to-the-dogs.

6. Mary Whitley, "Earmark Reform? Stimulus Bill Contains
9,000," *Cleveland Plain-Dealer*, February 22, 2009, http://www
.cleveland.com/nation/index.ssf/2009/02 /earmark_reform_stimulus
_bill_c.html.

7. "Obama: 'We're Out of Money,'" May 23, 2009 on Real
Clear Politics. http://www.realclearpolitics.com/video/2009/05/23
/obama_were_out_of_money.html. It is on YouTube at http://www
.youtube.com/watch?v=NQ4 RU9rlnbM.

8. Philip Elliott, "New Obama plans: 'spend our way out' of
downturn" Associated Press, December 8, 2009.

9. "Pelosi Says Republican Budget 'Out of Whack,'" May
17, 2006, House Democratic Leader Nancy Pelosi news release,
http://www.emailthecongress.com/news/ 2006/05-17-pelosi-says
-republican-budget-out-of-whack.

10. Stephen Moore, *How Barack Obama Is Bankrupting the
U.S. Economy* (New York: Encounter Books, 2009), 14–15.

11. David Dickson, "U.S. Red Ink Flirts with Crisis, Panel
Warns," *Washington Times*, December 15, 2009.

12. Charles Krauthammer, "An Anniversary of Sorts,"
Washington Post, December 18, 2009.

13. Brian S. Wesbury, *It's Not as Bad as You Think: Why
Capitalism Trumps Fear and the Economy Will Thrive* (Hoboken,
NJ: John Wiley & Sons, 2010), 188–89.

14. Steve Forbes and Elizabeth Ames, *How Capitalism Will
Save Us* (New York: Crown Business, 2009), 154.

15. Frederick M. Hess, "Soaring School Spending," American
Enterprise Institute, http://www.aei.org/issue /20303.

16. Andrew Roberts, "While America Slept," *American
Spectator*, February 2010, 22.

17. Charles Murray, "The Europe Syndrome and the Challenge to American Exceptionalism," the *American*, March 16, 2009.

18. Frederick Jackson Turner, *The Frontier in American History* (New York: Henry Holt and Company, 1921), passim.

AFTERWORD

1. David Carr and Tim Arango, "A Fox Chief at the Pinnacle of Media and Politics," *New York Times*, January 10, 2010.

2. Gabriel Sherman, "The Courtship: The story Behind the Obama-Brooks Bromance," *New Republic*, August 31, 2009, http://www.tnr.com/article/politics /the-courtship.

ACKNOWLEDGMENTS

Writers frequently make writing out to be a dreadful ordeal and writing a book the most dreadful ordeal of all. That fine *New York Times* sportswriter from days gone by, Red Smith, famously declared, "Writing is easy, you just sit down at the typewriter, open a vein and bleed it out drop by drop." Well, I would agree that for many writers putting their thoughts to paper is a kind of self-mutilation, and they ought to resist the temptation. For some of us, on the other hand, writing is actually quite pleasant.

As for writing an entire book, even so exuberant a man as Churchill descends from celebrating it as "an adventure," then "a toy and an amusement," to lamenting that "then it becomes a mistress, and then it becomes a master, and then a tyrant. The last phase is that just as you are about to be reconciled to your servitude, you kill the monster, and fling him out to the public."

In writing this book I never got beyond the amusement

phase. After all, this is a book about contemporary politics. As for mistresses, masters, and tyrants, my wife, Jeanne, maintains a .357 Magnum in the cupboard. So stand clear. I want to thank her for the security she supplies and so much more. With her nearby, writing this book was mostly a pleasure. I also want to acknowledge the friendship and assistance of others.

Alexander Hoyt, my agent, has assisted me with his keen literary sense and good judgment. So has Al Regnery, the publisher of the *American Spectator* and author of an indispensable history of modern American conservatism, *Upstream: The Ascendance of American Conservatism*. Al is also an important participant in the Conservative Action Project, a group that is becoming a major factor in the conservatives' recrudescence. *American Spectator* staffers, Jim Antle, Phil Klein, Joe Lawler, and Brian O'Connell have been generous in assisting me with research in their off-hours, as has my son, P. D. Tyrrell, once again. Two other staffers, Conn Martin and Katherine Ruddy, have assisted me generously in organizational matters. I am particularly grateful for the research talents of Mark Horne, provided for me by my splendid editor at Thomas Nelson, Joel Miller.

As a Media Fellow at the Hoover Institution, I have had available to me the stupendous research facilities of that great think tank, as well as access to its fine scholars. Several distinguished writers and scholars have advised me on sections of this book, among them, Herb London of the Hudson Institute, Myron Magnet of the Manhattan

Institute, and James Piereson of the William E. Simon Foundation. Jed Babbin, the editor of conservatism's oldest national publication, *Human Events*, advised on several sections of this book, as did Chuck Brunie, the Chairman of the Board of the *American Spectator*. While on the subject of the *AmSpec* board, let me express my gratitude to all the famously flinty members of that board, who appreciate the importance of a growing conservative counterculture. I am grateful for their support and counsel.

Finally, let me express my debt to the magazine's editorial director Wladyslaw Pleszczynski for his around-the-clock availability. John Von Kannon, now vice president and treasurer of the Heritage Foundation and once the *American Spectator*'s first publisher, verified events from the hazy past, as did Bill Kristol, founder and editor of the *Weekly Standard*. I want to express thanks to Alex Donner, to my longtime assistant Miss Myrna Larfnik, who assisted me even during a prolonged stay in hospital, and to Seth Lipsky, whose invaluable *The Citizen's Constitution: An Annotated Guide* has been very useful in apprising me of constitutional issues raised in the course of today's political struggles. Tom Wolfe also deserves my gratitude for his salutary influence on American culture during particularly parched times. Journalism and literature have benefited from his colossal gifts but also what Jacques Barzun once called the House of Intellect. To me he has been a generous friend and wise and worldly consultant.

No, writing this book has not been an ordeal. It has

been a stimulating intellectual exercise crowned I believe by a happy ending. As for Red Smith's recollections of lost blood, the only blood I am aware of spilling in the process of writing this book was not mine.

RET

ABOUT THE AUTHOR

R. Emmett Tyrrell Jr. is the founder and editor-in-chief of the famous and feared *American Spectator*, a political and cultural monthly published since he founded it as a college student in 1967. Bob's previous books include the *New York Times* best-selling *Boy Clinton, Madame Hillary, The Liberal Crack-Up*, and *The Conservative Crack-Up*. He makes frequent appearances on national television and is a nationally syndicated columnist whose articles have appeared in such publications as the *Wall Street Journal, New York Times, Los Angeles Times, Baltimore Sun, Washington Times, National Review, Harper's, Commentary, The (London) Spectator*, and *Le Figaro (Paris)*. Bob also serves as an adjunct fellow of the Hudson Institute and a contributing editor to the New York Sun.

Visit the American Spectator online: Spectator.org

INDEX

A

abortion, 5, 6, 9, 47, 147
Abramoff, Jack, 48–49, 63, 193, 231
ABSCAM, 49
Acheson, Dean, 138, 141, 143
ACORN (Association of Community Organizations for Reform Now), 120–21
administration (presidential): Bush (G. H. W.), 137; Bush (G. W.), 17, 19, 39, 65, 91, 100, 110, 112–13, 133, 167, 190–91, 193, 206, 231; Carter, 60, 78; Clinton, 9, 19, 65, 154, 182; Kennedy, 115; Nixon, 62, 73, 75–77, 79, 184, 230; Obama, xii, 42, 119–20, 135, 172, 202–5, 233; Reagan, 4, 37, 38, 43, 75, 81, 94–95, 114, 115, 131, 138, 149, 167, 187, 190, 191, 208, 222; Roosevelt, 114, 132, 137, 141; Truman, 137
affirmative action, 188
Age of Reagan: A History, 1974–2008, The (Wilentz), 44
Agnew, Spiro T., 229
airport screenings, 220
Alinsky, Saul, 42
Al-Qaeda, 223

American Civil Liberties Union (ACLU), 180
American Conservative Union (ACU), 71, 129
American Enterprise Institute (AEI), 38, 168, 170, 184–85, 190, 195, 196
American exceptionalism, 202, 224–26
American Recovery and Reinvestment Act of 2009 ($787 billion stimulus package), 204–5
Americans for Tax Reform, 113, 195
American Spectator, 4, 38, 48, 56, 64, 77, 78, 105–9, 111, 167, 182, 195, 211, 223, 258–59
Americans for Democratic Action (ADA), 36, 71, 136–37
Anderson, Martin, 76, 79, 83
antitrust reform, 196
Annan, Noel, 15
anti-Communists, 71, 130, 134, 136–37, 139, 144–45, 154, 155, 161, 192
Aristotle, 34, 70
Armey, Dick, 113, 190, 194
Atlas Economic Research Foundation, 169
Atlantic magazine, 40
"axis of evil," 39

INDEX

INDEX

Pew Charitable Trusts (Glenmede Trust, in text), 176–77, 178
philanthropy, 174, 176–81, 187–88
Pickens, T. Boone (Pickens Plan), 218–19
Piereson, James, 95, 98, 122, 173, 174, 178, 187–89, 259
Pinochet, Augusto, 176
Pleszczynski, Wladyslaw, 38, 259
Podhoretz, Norman, 78, 81–82
Policy Review (quarterly), 102, 109
Politico (online magazine), 37
populism, 33–34
presidential election: of 1980, 82, 231; 1984, 75; 1992, 10; 2000, 20–21, 44, 99; 2004, 12, 46; 2008, 3, 18, 26–27, 32–33, 35, 40, 44, 46, 47–48, 112, 195
Public Interest (quarterly), 77, 82, 109
Pulitzer Prize, 26, 101, 115

Q

quotas, 151: gender and racial, 150, 151, 188–89

R

racism, 33, 37, 43, 44, 117, 148, 149, 249
Read, Leonard, 175
Reagan, Nancy, 79–80
Reagan, Ronald, 4, 5–7, 9–10, 38, 53, 64, 70, 72, 74, 75–76, 78, 79, 80–83, 100, 103–4, 109, 113, 114, 138, 173, 174, 185, 189, 195, 202, 203, 207, 208, 221, 222, 226, 229, 230, 231. See also administration (presidential): Reagan
Reagan I Knew, The (Buckley Jr.), 32
"Reagan Democrats," 147, 161, 192
Reagan Revolution, 60, 146, 154, 202
reason, xvi, 89, 131, 149, 151, 159, 163
Red Scare, 96–97, 138, 144, 145
Reformed Conservatives (RCs), 35–36, 38, 44, 47, 67, 68, 92, 117–18, 124, 133, 160, 173, 194, 207, 231, 232

Regnery Publishing, 64, 135
Regnery, Al, 63–64, 72, 195, 258
Regnery, Henry, 135, 136
Reich, Charles, 60
Relm Foundation, 177
Republican Party (GOP), 20, 32, 39, 40–41, 44, 46, 49, 74, 78, 90, 189
Republican takeover of Congress (1994), 35
Reuther, Walter, 137
Reynolds, David, 145
Right Nation, The (Micklethwait and Wooldridge), 12, 13, 106, 111
Road to Serfdom, The (Hayek), 159, 168, 170–72
Roberts, Andrew, 224–25
Rockefeller, Nelson, 73
Rockefeller Brothers Fund, 177
Rockefeller Foundation, 177, 178
Roosevelt, Eleanor, 73
Roosevelt, Franklin D. (FDR), 7, 22, 103, 114, 135, 201. *See also* administration (presidential): Roosevelt
Rose, Charlie, 56
Rove, Karl, 39
Rusher, William, 71

S

Safire, William, 230
Scaife, Richard M., 178–84
Scaife, Sarah, 180
Scarborough, Joe, 123–24
Schlesinger, Arthur M., Jr., 15, 115, 130–32, 134, 136–37, 153
school choice, 190
"Scoop" Jackson Democrats, 185
Scranton, William, 73
sectionalism, 33
September 11, 2001 (9/11), 120, 201, 221, 222
Sessions, Jeff, 36–37, 117
Shakespeare, Frank, 73
Sharon Statement, 63
Sherwood, Robert, 114–15
Silicon Valley, 91, 174
60 Minutes, 56

INDEX

Smith, Adam, 170, 175
Smith Richardson Foundation, 178
socialism, xii, 169, 172, 196
Social Security, 190, 196, 206, 212
Sorensen, Ted, 26
Sotomayor, Sonia, 36
Soviet Union, 78, 81, 96, 103, 139,
    143, 208
stagflation, 92, 209
statism, 160, 169
Steinbeck, John, 115
Stigler, George, 170, 175
stimulus bill. See American Recovery
    and Reinvestment Act of 2009
Strauss, Leo, 170
Students for a Democratic Society
    (SDS), 71
Sunstein, Cass, 94–95, 110, 192
supply-side economics, 82, 92, 98,
    100, 189, 196
Supreme Court (U.S.). See United
    States Supreme Court

T

Taft, Robert A., 7, 8, 54
talk radio, 33, 109, 123–24, 128–29,
    167, 232
Tammany Hall, 49
Tanenhaus, Sam, 48
tax cuts, 80, 92, 100, 151, 189, 192,
    211
tax reform, 39, 209, 210–11
Taylor, Zachary, 103
Tea Party, 121, 194
telecommunications, 220
terrorists, 42, 201, 220, 222
Thatcher, Margaret, 64, 102, 169,
    173, 189, 193
Theodoracopulos, Taki, 56
Thomas, Clarence, 105, 110–11
Thomson, Virgil, 115
Thrift Savings Plan, 212
Thurmond, Strom, 148
Today Show, 183
tort reform, 196–97, 214, 216
"traditional conservatives," 91

traditionalists: emphasis of, 158–59
Troopergate, 105–6
Truman, Harry, 136, 137, 138, 144
Turner, Frederick Jackson, 226
Twain, Mark, 43
Tyrrell Doctrine, 223–24

U

unemployment, 100, 208–9
United States Constitution, 35, 90,
    132, 155, 159, 162, 172, 186, 218
United States House of Representatives,
    17, 45, 46
United States Supreme Court, 5, 36,
    45, 105, 111
University of Chicago, 26, 127,
    175–76
"unreasonable searches and seizures,"
    220
Up from Liberalism (Buckley), xiii
USA Today, 46, 47, 98

V

Van Natta, Don, 106
"vast right-wing conspiracy," 98, 101,
    176, 183
Venona project, 96–97, 143–45
Vietnam War, 21, 34, 138
Voegelin, Eric, 170
Volker, William, 169, 174, 177, 177
Volker Fund, 169, 170, 174–75, 177
von Mises, Ludwig, 135, 175

W

Wallace, George, 147
Wallace, Henry, 137, 141–42
Wallace, Mike, 56
Wall Street Journal, 38, 109, 195
Washington conventional wisdom, 13,
    17, 18–19, 23, 44–47
Washington Post, 17, 98, 109, 110,
    120, 122, 182, 183, 232
Washington Times, 38, 109
Watergate, 23, 75
weapons of mass destruction, 98, 99,
    100, 201, 220